This book is a valuable int̶̶̶̶
and persuasive theologian. For t̶h̶o̶s̶e̶
he stood on the great themes of Christian tru̶t̶h̶,
excellent place to begin.

Gerald Bray
Research Professor of Divinity, Beeson Divinity School
Author of *God is Love: A Biblical and Systematic Theology*

Readers of this book will happily learn much about Augustine, because the writing has the temper of coming from a scholar who has become Augustine's friend. We are formed and shaped by the friends we spend time with. Given the vicissitudes, challenges and superficialities of today's culture and Church, one of the best tonics is to spend time learning how to love anew. Augustine remains one of our most reliable guides to the heart. This book enables us to enjoy sharing in Augustine's insights that Prof. Green treasures.

Peter Sanlon
Author of *Augustine's Theology of Preaching*

Augustine is the great formative influence on Western theology. Anyone seriously interested in that theology cannot afford to neglect him. In this book, Bradley Green offers to readers a well-researched, thoughtful, and straightforward introductory guide to the main elements in Augustine's mind and writings, from which any student of historical theology can profit. I will be urging my students to utilize it. The Augustinian heritage is a deep and precious one in many areas, often ignorantly and unjustly criticized; one more solid contribution to the exploration and commendation of that heritage is always a very welcome item.

Nick Needham
Church History lecturer, Highland Theological College, Dingwall, Scotland
Author of the series *2000 Years of Christ's Power*

Brad Green has produced a delightful book on a gigantically complex and important person in the history of Christianity and western culture. His treatment of Augustine isolates the most pertinent citations on the most important and formative parts of the Augustinian corpus. Not only does the reader receive a condensed course in Augustinian theology, but also the theological observations of Green himself in the necessary judgments that arise from engagement with the provocative texts of Augustine. Green's personal observations are astute and theologically instructive. He effectively referees the relation between Augustine as a shaper of the Protestant Reformation and as a doctor of the Roman Catholic Church. The book is manageable, concise, clear, accurate, and pleasant to read. His suggestions for reading Augustine are a treasure in themselves.

Tom J. Nettles

Professor of Historical Theology, The Southern Baptist Theological Seminary, Louisville, Kentucky

Brad Green had the bright idea of writing a short book on the life and accomplishments of the greatest of theologians, Augustine of Hippo. The book, is clear, well-organised and compact. Brad tells the reader not only of the great man himself, but how to read his well-known books and to cherish them. The difficult issues are not shirked, covering everything between classical theism and Donatism. He consults not only primary sources, the writings, but also apt comments on the great man, secondary materials. The ideal start-up companion.

Paul Helm

Formerly Professor of the History and Philosophy of Religion, King's College, London

EARLY CHURCH FATHERS
SERIES EDITORS
MICHAEL A. G. HAYKIN & SHAWN J. WILHITE

AUGUSTINE
OF HIS LIFE & IMPACT
HIPPO

BRADLEY G. GREEN

CHRISTIAN
FOCUS

Copyright © Bradley G. Green 2020

Bradley G. Green has asserted his right under the Copyright, Designs and Patents Act, 1988, to be identified as Author of this work.

paperback ISBN 978-1-5271-0587-4
epub ISBN 978-1-5271-0653-6
mobi ISBN 978-1-5271-0654-3

First published in 2020
Reprinted in 2021
by
Christian Focus Publications Ltd,
Geanies House, Fearn, Ross-shire.
IV20 1TW, Scotland.
www.christianfocus.com
A CIP catalogue record for this book is available from the British Library.

Cover designer: MOOSE77

Printed by Bell and Bain, Glasgow.

MIX
Paper from
responsible sources
FSC
www.fsc.org FSC® C007785

CONTENTS

FOREWORD

As a young student, I approached the great Augustine not only by exposing myself to his writings (*The Confessions* and select portions of *The City of God* to start with), but also through the masterful (and Roman Catholic) introductions by Etienne Gilson and Agostino Trapè. These are monuments of twentieth-century scholarship and substantial studies in the field. Their comprehensive reading of Augustine, though recognizing areas of theological tension within the church father, underlined the overall harmony of his theology and his alignment with what Roman Catholicism would have subsequently held on to in terms of its doctrine and practice. In later years, when reading the Protestant Reformers, I encountered a different reading of Augustine, one which prioritized the solidity and pervasiveness of his theology of grace and, at the same time, acknowledged serious inconsistencies with it, especially in his ecclesiology. B. B. Warfield described the conundrum as 'two children struggling in the womb of his mind,' with the Protestant Reformation finally suggesting that the real Augustine is that of his doctrine of grace.

This is to say that there are significantly different interpretations of Augustine. How then do we approach Augustine's universe, given the pivotal and towering importance of his legacy on Western theology and culture, together with the complex task of dealing with a theology of such scope?

For sure, introductions to Augustine abound. One can think of Peter Brown's, Henry Chadwick's, or Henri Marrou's classics on Augustine. Yet today the introductory studies on Augustine are graced with a new, impressive addition. I welcome this volume by Dr. Bradley Green. This book has all the credibility necessary to become a useful and reliable guide to the noted church father for years ahead. Green stands on a rich tradition of contemporary Evangelical Protestant studies of Augustine: David Wright, Gerald Bray, and Nick Needham are just a few scholars who have explored Augustine's world and have helped students and thoughtful readers to navigate it. This volume makes the voice of Augustine audible through the many quotations that are fairly discussed and assessed throughout. It also guides the reader to come to terms with the biblical richness, theological depth, and remaining oddities of one of the greatest minds in the history of the Christian church.

Leonardo De Chirico

Lecturer of Historical Theology—Istituto di Formazione Evangelica e Documentazione (Padova, Italy) and Director of the Reformanda Initiative (Rome, Italy)

SERIES PREFACE

On reading the Church Fathers

By common definition, the Church Fathers are those early Christian authors who wrote between the close of the first century, right after the death of the last of the apostles—namely the apostle John—and the middle of the eighth century. In other words, those figures who were active in the life of the church between Ignatius of Antioch and Clement of Rome, who penned writings at the very beginning of the second century, and the Venerable Bede and John of Damascus, who stood at the close of antiquity and the onset of the Middle Ages. Far too many evangelicals in the modern day know next to nothing about these figures. I will never forget being asked to give a mini-history conference at a church in southern Ontario. I suggested three talks on three figures from Latin-speaking North Africa: Perpetua, Cyprian, and Augustine. The leadership of the church came back to me seeking a different set of names, since they had never heard of the first two figures, and while they had heard of the third name, the famous bishop of Hippo Regius, they really knew nothing about him. I gave them another list of post-Reformation figures for the mini-conference, but privately thought that not knowing anything about these figures was possibly a very good reason to have a conference on them! I suspect that such ignorance is quite widespread among those who call themselves Evangelicals—hence the importance of this small series of studies on a select number of Church Fathers, to educate and inform God's people about their forebears in the faith.

Past appreciation for the Fathers

How different is the modern situation from the past, when many of our Evangelical and Reformed forebears knew and treasured the writings of the ancient church. The French Reformer John Calvin, for example, was ever a keen student of the Church Fathers. He did not always agree with them, even when it came to one of his favorite authors, namely, Augustine. But he was deeply aware of the value of knowing their thought and drawing upon the riches of their written works for elucidating the Christian faith in his own day. And in the seventeenth century, the Puritan theologian John Owen, rightly called the 'Calvin of England' by some of his contemporaries, was not slow to turn to the experience of the one he called 'holy Austin,' namely Augustine, to provide him with a pattern of God the Holy Spirit's work in conversion.

Yet again, when the Particular Baptist John Gill was faced with the anti-Trinitarianism of the Deist movement in the early eighteenth century, and other Protestant bodies—for instance, the English Presbyterians, the General Baptists, and large tracts of Anglicanism—were unable to retain a firm grasp on this utterly vital biblical doctrine, Gill turned to the Fathers to help him elucidate the biblical teaching regarding the blessed Trinity. Gill's example in this regard influenced other Baptists such as John Sutcliff, pastor of the Baptist cause in Olney, where John Newton also ministered. Sutcliff was so impressed by the

Letter to Diognetus, which he wrongly supposed to have been written by Justin Martyr, that he translated it for The Biblical Magazine, a Calvinistic publication with a small circulation. He sent it to the editor of this periodical with the commendation that this second-century work is 'one of the most valuable pieces of ecclesiastical antiquity.'

One final caveat

One final word about the Fathers recommended in this small series of essays. The Fathers are not Scripture. They are senior conversation partners about Scripture and its meaning. We listen to them respectfully, but are not afraid to disagree when they err. As the Reformers rightly argued, the writings of the Fathers must be subject to Scripture. John Jewel, the Anglican apologist, put it well when he stated in 1562:

> But what say we of the fathers, Augustine, Ambrose, Jerome, Cyprian, etc.? What shall we think of them, or what account may we make of them? They be interpreters of the word of God. They were learned men, and learned fathers; the instruments of the mercy of God, and vessels full of grace. We despise them not, we read them, we reverence them, and give thanks unto God for them. They were witnesses unto the truth, they were worthy pillars and ornaments in the church of God. Yet may they not be compared with the word of God. We may not build upon them: we may not make them the foundation and warrant of our conscience: we may not put our trust in them. Our trust is in the name of the Lord.

Michael A. G. Haykin and Shawn J. Wilhite
The Southern Baptist Theological Seminary
Louisville, Kentucky

INTRODUCTION

As a theological student, I knew Augustine was someone I ought to read. But as often happens, it was a personal or existential need that finally drove me to Augustine (fitting, indeed, as those who have read the *Confessions* will know). While in graduate school, I was trying to come to terms with 'postmodernism' and 'modernism' and the question of language, including whether and how language could be a true medium of meaning. I was trying to make sense of structuralism, post-structuralism, deconstruction, Jacques Derrida, and more.

I had picked up *Confessions* years before but, for whatever reason, it did not grab me. But in the middle of my wrestling with the nature of so-called postmodernism, I took a *Confessions* seminar as part of my Ph.D. work. During this seminar I of course read *Confessions*, but was even more taken with *On Christian Doctrine* and *The Teacher*, for in both of these works Augustine was forging a Christian understanding of language—just what I was looking for. I have continued my fascination with Augustine ever since, including a doctoral dissertation with significant portions dealing with his thought.

Some Commitments and Goals

Let me share some of my goals for this book, as well as some of my commitments, with the reader.

First, as I began to lay out my writing and reading agenda, and to think through how to structure the book, one thought kept pressing itself upon me: I want to write a book that *I* would hand to someone who asked: 'What would you recommend to me if I wanted to begin to understand Augustine?' Life is too short for 'just another book' on Augustine. So, I hope you find that this is a book about which you can say: 'It gave me a good overview of who Augustine was and what he thought.'

Second, this book is written by someone committed to the theological perspective of the Protestant Reformation. Rather than be coy or even duplicitous, it is best to be straightforward on this point. It is commonplace to quote B. B. Warfield, who said that the Reformation was the victory of Augustine's doctrine of grace over his doctrine of the church. We will return to this maxim later. But throughout this volume, we will have an eye on how a Protestant is to understand Augustine. I hope this will illuminate Augustine's thought rather than obscure it (and I am optimistic on this point!). There are perhaps two types of errors Evangelicals can commit.

First, we can engage in *unnecessary denigration* of the patristic tradition, in which anything from that era is viewed with such suspicion that it never is really given a fair hearing, and the contemporary church is robbed of many wonderful insights.

Or second, we can engage in *unnecessary hagiography*, in which the patristic tradition is simply embraced as always getting it right, and the patristic era is seen as the golden era—with all post-patristic theologizing seen as a fall from a pristine theological Eden.

In what follows we will attempt to avoid both of these trajectories (obviously painted with simplicity, and somewhat exaggerated to make the point). Instead, we will engage the thought of Augustine, first and foremost, by trying to understand him. Along the way we will query how a Protestant should think of Augustine. The discoveries should be very interesting indeed. Since Augustine lived and wrote over one thousand years before Protestant-Catholic polemics, he obviously was not trying to craft his words to speak to this or that controversy *in the particular ways they would play themselves out in the age of the Reformation*. We will look at many issues—and we will not dodge the particularly fascinating ones like justification, the nature of Scripture and its relationship to tradition, and the nature of baptism and the Lord's Supper. We will find three kinds of relationship between Augustinian and Protestant thought:

1. At times the Protestant will find in Augustine a way of articulating things which can be appropriated with little change or concern.
2. At times the Protestant will find in Augustine a way of articulating things which is more puzzling or troubling, and must be re-worked before really being appropriated.
3. At times the Protestant will find in Augustine a way of articulating things which really should not and cannot be appropriated.

Third, my goal is to write out of a (hopefully!) rich understanding of Augustine, but not in a way that is unduly technical or difficult. So, I hope this book will be accessible and helpful to any person willing to work a bit at reading and understanding.

Fourth, in a book of this sort it is always tempting to try to 'get Augustine on one's side.' For example, one French Catholic wrote: 'To have [St. Augustine] on one's side is tantamount to having the doctrine of the Church and the Gospel in one's favor.'[1] There is indeed a temptation to approach Augustine

---

1   This quotation is from Henri de Lubac, *Augustinianism and Modern Theology*, translated by Louis Dupré (New York: Herder and Herder, 2000), xix n7. De Lubac is quoting J. Leporcq from the preface of Leporcq's *Sentiments de saint Augustin sur la grâce* (no publication information given).

in this way, but this book will try to avoid succumbing to this potential pitfall.

While I was writing this book friends often asked me, 'So, have you read all that Augustine has written?' In case you are curious, the answer is 'no.' But I take comfort from Isidore of Seville, who is reported to have said: 'If anyone told you he had read all the works of Augustine, he was a liar.'[2]

The book concludes with an annotated bibliography and suggestions for further study. There is no reason to be intimidated at the prospect of reading Augustine. One might simply say, 'Start anywhere!' (not the worst advice). But in this section I will offer guidance to the reader who would like to explore Augustine further but is not quite sure where to begin.

---

2   This quotation is traced to Peter Brown, 'Political Society,' in Richard Markus, ed. *Augustine: A Collection of Critical Essays* (Garden City, N.J.: Doubleday, 1972), 311. I found it in Jean Bethke Elshtain, 'Why Augustine? Why Now?,' in *Augustine and Postmodernism: Confessions and Circumfession*, edited by John D. Caputo and Michael J. Scanlon (Bloomington, IN: Indiana University Press, 2005), 255–56. Isidore of Seville was a Spanish theologian who lived from 560 to 636. Isidore is often called the 'last' of the church fathers.

1

THE LIFE OF AUGUSTINE

'Take and read.' 'Wherever one finds truth, it is the Lord's.' 'You have made us for yourself, O Lord, and our hearts are restless until they find their rest in thee.' These sayings—and many others—come from the pen of Aurelius Augustinus, known to us today as Augustine. He is unarguably one of the greatest theologians in the history of the Christian church, and arguably the most significant. Who was this man whom Henry Chadwick could call 'the greatest figure of Christian antiquity'?[1]

Augustine (A.D. 354-430) is what we call today a 'Western' theologian—in that he spoke and wrote in Latin and lived and worked in the western half of Christendom. He was born in the small town of Thagaste in northern Africa on November 13, 354 (present-day Souk-Ahras, in Algeria). Augustine's father Patricius does not appear to have been a Christian, but he was committed to his son and to providing a good education for him. Augustine's mom was indeed a confessing Christian and is portrayed by Augustine as zealously committed to her son's spiritual wellbeing, and as praying fervently for him during his rather debauched youth.

---

1   Henry Chadwick, in his foreword to Serge Lancel, *St. Augustine*, tr. Antonia Nevill (London: SCM, 2002), 14.

It is difficult to come to terms with Augustine's 'life' without having some understanding of his spiritual, theological, and philosophical pilgrimage. We will consider this in some detail below, as well as the key controversies that indelibly shaped him.

Augustine was classically educated, in that he studied the trivium—the 'language arts' of grammar, logic or dialectic, and rhetoric (i.e., the 'three ways' of the classical liberal arts). He studied in Madouros (near Thagaste), and then, after a year of idleness in Thagaste (369-70), he moved to Carthage for further study (370-73). It is here that Augustine discovered a work by the first-century B.C. Roman orator and statesman Cicero: *Hortensius*. Interestingly, this text ignites a love for wisdom in Augustine. In God's mysterious and sovereign way, He uses this Roman orator as one piece of the mosaic of Augustine's life that would culminate in devotion to the love of wisdom.

Augustine's reflections on his own educational experience are fascinating. Many today look to Augustine as a model for exemplary classical education. This is understandable, but as Augustine worked through the varied implications of being a Christian, his own reflections on his educational background are quite mixed. As noted above, Augustine did indeed study what are often called the liberal arts—especially the so-called trivium of grammar, dialectic (roughly equal to logic), and rhetoric. But as Augustine reflects on his own traditional education, and does so explicitly as a Christian, he offers significant criticism of it.

Augustine reflected at some length on what a more Christian approach to language or rhetoric might look like—especially in his *On Christian Doctrine*. As a Christian, Augustine's mind had turned to eternal, spiritual, and ultimate things, and he lamented that much of his formal education was not concerned in the least with such realities. It was not that Augustine—as a Christian— rejected such everyday things such as education. Rather, it is probably truer to say that Augustine began to *reconfigure* or *reinterpret* the nature, practice, and ends of education in light of his Christian conversion.

Thus Augustine says: 'See the exact care with which the sons of men observe the conventions of letters and syllables received from those who so talked before them.'[2] He continues: 'Yet they neglect the eternal contracts of lasting salvation received from you.' That is, some people are particularly concerned with getting the 'letters and syllables' correct, but they are *not* attentive to the salvific words that proceed from God Himself. Likewise, Augustine criticizes anyone who 'is extremely vigilant in precautions against some error in language, but is indifferent to the possibility that the emotional force of his mind may bring about a man's execution.'[3] The problem is clear: one can know grammar and rhetoric but be indifferent to the most egregious of moral problems.

Augustine makes a series of striking comments related to his own classical education in the trivium. He first speaks of his own training in 'literature and oratory' which his father was eager to fund. Augustine laments that while many people praised his father for sacrificing to provide his son a superior education in the language arts, his father possessed no analogous commitment to the training of Augustine's character: 'But this same father did not care what character before you I was developing, or how chaste I was so long as I possessed a cultured tongue—though my culture really meant a desert uncultivated by you, God. You are the one true and good lord of your land, which is my heart.'[4]

At times Augustine speaks positively of rhetoric in *Confessions*. But interestingly, he seems to consider himself something of a renegade in doing so! Unlike (in his telling) other teachers of rhetoric, Augustine sought to teach others the 'tricks of rhetoric'

2   *Confessions* I.27.29. Unless otherwise noted, I am utilizing Henry Chadwick's English translation of *Confessions* (Oxford: Oxford University Press, 1991).

3   *Ibid.*

4   *Ibid.*, II.3.5.

but 'without any resort to a trick.' And he did this 'not that they should use them *against* the life of an innocent man, but that sometimes they might save the life of a guilty person.' Augustine believed that God saw in Augustine 'the spark of my integrity,' which prompted him to teach rhetoric with an aim to a virtuous goal. [5]

Augustine does speak of 'eloquence' (*eloquentia*) in Book X, [6] but mainly as a study in contrasts between how we recall something like happiness or joy and how we recall eloquence. [7] In recounting his own education in rhetoric, Augustine sometimes speaks of textbooks on eloquence but here he is lamenting his own sin, and what drove him to study in the first place. He writes: 'I wanted to distinguish myself as an orator for a damnable and conceited purpose, namely delight in human vanity.' [8]

Augustine evaluates positively Moses' 'skill in eloquence' and his 'facility of style.' [9] But what is the advantage to such training in the liberal arts, if Augustine is 'the most wicked slave of evil lusts'? [10] Intellectual and mental acuity are gifts, Augustine affirms, 'but that did not move me to offer them [i.e., such gifts] to you.' [11] Augustine asks poignantly: 'What advantage did it bring me to have a good thing and not to use it well?' [12] Augustine confesses that although he might have excelled in the liberal arts, he could nonetheless at the time affirm various egregious heresies. Thus:

> What profit, then, was it for me at that time that my agile mind found no difficulty in these subjects, and that without assistance from a human teacher I could elucidate extremely

---

5   *Ibid.*, IV.2.2.

6   *Ibid.*, X.21.30

7   *Ibid.*

8   *Ibid.*, III.4.7.

9   *Ibid.*, XII.26.36.

10   *Ibid.*, IV.16.30.

11   *Ibid.*

12   *Ibid.*, IV.16.39

complicated books, when my comprehension of religion was erroneous, distorted, and shamefully sacrilegious?[13]

It was also in Carthage that Augustine encountered and eventually 'joined' (or was associated with) the Manicheans.[14] The Manicheans were a dualistic and gnostic sect that had its origins in the third century A.D. in Persia (modern-day Iran) with a man named Mani. Augustine would remain enmeshed in Manichaeism for nine years.

The Manicheans believed that at one point Spirit and Matter, Good and Evil, Light and Dark, had all been separated from one another. However, these things had become mixed together, so that this dualism runs through the heart of all things—including human beings. Hence, to be 'saved' is to be released or rescued from materiality, which was considered to be intrinsically evil—hence the gnostic flavor to Manicheism, since gnosticism posits that physical 'stuff' is inherently bad or evil. Augustine eventually became disillusioned with Manicheism, especially after one of their famed teachers was unable to satisfactorily address some of his intellectual dilemmas. In Carthage Augustine would also take a concubine. They would have one child together, a son named Adeodatus (Latin for 'given by God'), who was born in 372.

Augustine spent a year in Rome (383–84) and then went to Milan, where he met Ambrose, the bishop. Augustine taught rhetoric in Milan, but more importantly, perhaps, he came under the influence of Ambrose during this time. Augustine also developed a circle of friends and discovered the books of the Platonists. If we think of Cicero's *Hortensius* and Manicheism as the first two most important intellectual influences in

---

13   *Ibid.*, IX.16.31. Augustine also briefly deals with rhetoric or eloquence in *Confessions* IV.14.21 and V.23.13.

14   I put 'joined' in quotes because one would become more and more 'in' the Manichees over time, and Augustine was never in the inner circle in the fullest sense.

Augustine's life, then the books of the Platonists are the third, sequentially. Augustine refers to this discovery explicitly in his *Confessions*.

When Augustine speaks of the Platonists he is referring to what we now call the 'Neo-Platonists,' a development or form of Platonism seen in thinkers like Plotinus (A.D. 204–270) and Porphyry (A.D. 234–305). Neo-Platonism is 'Platonic' in that it privileges the immaterial over the material, but unlike Manicheism it does not see the material world as inherently evil. Thus Neo-Platonism seems to have given Augustine some tools, or at least a viable framework, for thinking of the created order as good—an affirmation that would of course be necessary as Augustine worked out his own theological convictions. Augustine would write in *Confessions* that he was 'on fire' reading the books of the Platonists. While Augustine later labored to extricate himself from those aspects of Neoplatonism that were less friendly to Christian belief, he arguably never fully separated himself from Neoplatonism as a system or worldview.

In 385, Augustine's mother Monica arranged a marriage for him. In Monica's view Augustine was destined for great things, and his current mistress simply would not do. Augustine ultimately sent his mistress back to North Africa, keeping Adeodatus with him. Little is known about the mother of Augustine's son. He eventually separated from her, and does not seem to mention her in his large corpus other than in the *Confessions*:

> The woman with whom I habitually slept was torn away from my side because she was a hindrance to my marriage. My heart which was deeply attached was a hindrance to my marriage [i.e., the marriage planned by Augustine's mom, Monica]. My heart which was deeply attached was cut and wounded, and left a trail of blood. She had returned to Africa vowing that she would

never go with another man. She left with me the natural son I had by her.[15]

Augustine's planned marriage was to take place in a couple of years, but it never occurred. After the mother of his son had departed, but before the scheduled and planned marriage, Augustine took another lover:

> I was unhappy, incapable of following a woman's example, and impatient of delay. I was to get the girl I had proposed to only at the end of two years. As I was not a lover of marriage but a slave of lust, I procured another woman, not of course as wife. By this liaison the disease of my soul would be sustained and kept active, either in full vigor or even increased, so that the habit would be guarded and fostered until I came to the kingdom of marriage. But my wound, inflicted by the earlier parting, was not healed. After inflammation and sharp pain, it festered. The pain made me as it were frigid and desperate.[16]

Lancel suggests that since Augustine's own sexual sins were so significant in his life, at some point Augustine essentially determined not to write or speak of the mother of Adeodatus: 'The *damnatio nominis*—the enforced forgetfulness of her name—was the heavy lid placed on his casket of memories.'[17]

The young woman Monica had chosen was indeed rather young, and thus it would be a while before the marriage could occur. In fact, the marriage never did occur. Augustine remained single for the rest of his days.

But perhaps Augustine's time in Milan is most remembered for his conversion, which takes place in a garden in that Italian city (A.D. 386). Augustine offers his own 'spiritual autobiography' in the *Confessions*. As he describes it, he had for a time harbored certain intellectual or even aesthetic quibbles with the Christian

---

15   *Confessions* VI.15.25.

16   *Ibid.*

17   Lancel, *Augustine*, 27.

faith. For example, the Old and New Testaments seemed rather crude, and lacking in classical form. Should not the very Word of God be written in a grander form? And what about evil? If the Christian God is truly all-powerful and all-good, how does one explain evil?

Over time, these intellectual or aesthetic objections were resolved for Augustine. Yet such a resolution only revealed that Augustine's objections to Christianity were deeper than even he had initially grasped. Augustine came to realize that he did not believe in Christianity because he *did not want* to believe. Readers are encouraged to read book (that is, chapter) eight of the *Confessions*. Augustine recounts that he was like someone asleep who wants to wake up, but simply cannot. Augustine prays his famous prayer: 'Grant me chastity and self-continence, but not yet.'[18] To make things worse, Augustine heard that Victorinus (a significant intellectual) had converted to Christianity. And so had Augustine's friend Alypius. Thus, Augustine's spiritual lethargy was now compounded with a kind of perverse jealousy!

In the midst of this Augustine, while in the garden in Milan, hears voices saying, 'Take, read!' (*tolle lege*). Augustine looks around to find out who is speaking. Is this some sort of children's game? He cannot discover the source. Then, he notices a Bible next to him on a bench, and turns to Romans 13, where he reads: 'Not in riots and drunken parties, not in eroticism and indecencies, not in strike and rivalry, but put on the Lord Jesus Christ and make no provision for the flesh in its lusts' (Rom. 3:13–14). Augustine writes in *Confessions*: 'I neither wished nor needed to read further. At once, with the last words of this sentence, it was as if a light of relief from all anxiety flooded into my heart. All the shadows of doubt were dispelled.'[19]

After his conversion Augustine resigned from teaching rhetoric. Augustine, his mother, his brother Navigius, his son

18   *Confessions* VIII.7.17.
19   *Ibid.*, VIII.12.29.

Adeodatus, his cousins Lartidianus and Rusticus, as well as Licentius (the son of a friend) all moved to Cassiciacum, a small town outside Milan. This was to be a place for friends to live and discuss central philosophical issues. During this period Augustine wrote three key works: *Against the Skeptics*, *The Happy Life*, and *On Order*.

It seems that Augustine was under some stress or perhaps was emotionally or personally agitated prior to his move to Cassiciacum. It was hoped that this life of leisure and philosophical discussion would help. But this hoped-for idyllic existence was not to last. Though not unhappy there, Augustine did not break free from—or find lasting relief from—his agitation or stress. Augustine thus returned to Milan in early 387, and was baptized by Ambrose. Augustine recounts his baptism and the joy that followed:

> We were baptized,[20] and disquiet about our past life vanished from us. During those days I found an insatiable and amazing delight in considering the profundity of your purpose for the salvation of the human race. How I wept during your hymns and songs! I was deeply moved by the music of the sweet chants of your Church. The sounds flowed into my ears and the truth was distilled into my heart. This caused the feelings of devotion to overflow. Tears ran, and it was good for me to have that experience.[21]

Later that year Augustine and his family and friends left Milan to head to Africa, stopping in Ostia for a while, where Monica died. Augustine then diverted his entourage to Rome instead of Africa, where Augustine wrote the anti-Manichean polemical works *Morals of the Catholic Church* and *Morals of the Manicheans*. Works such as *The Greatness of the Soul* and (parts of) *On Free Will* were written during this time (387–388).

---

20   Like often in our own day, a group of persons were baptized at the same time, or in the same service.

21   *Confessions* IX.6.14.

In the fall of 388 Augustine, his son Adeodatus, and his friends Evodius and Alypius returned to Africa. After a brief stay in Carthage, Augustine went to Thagaste. One writer notes that the house in Thagaste 'marks a transition between the studious villa at Cassiciacum and the monasteries properly speaking that will appear at Hippo.'[22] Augustine effectively liquidated his assets to form something of a Christian community in Thagaste. Augustine lived in his childhood home but appears to have given his various assets to the church.[23]

We learn something of the closeness of the friendship between Augustine and Nebridius from this time in Thagaste. His dear friend Nebridius was living roughly 170 miles away in the Carthaginian countryside. Nebridius desired to be nearer to Augustine and was saddened that Augustine seemed so tied to Thagaste that significant distance would continue to separate them. Due to the distance, Augustine and Nebridius engaged in extensive correspondence, which Lancel calls 'the most important among documents of this kind, and without doubt also the most moving.'[24] During this time in Thagaste, Augustine also had his friends Alypius, Evodius, and Severus with him.

Augustine continued to write, and undertook the first of his several attempts to wrestle with the text of Genesis: *On Genesis, against the Manichees*. He also wrote *On True Religion* (where Augustine explores the importance of 'happiness' in the life of a person) and *The Teacher* (where he considers how to think about 'signs'—a frequent concern of his that shows up again in *On Christian Doctrine*).

Like many talented Christians in the history of the Christian church, Augustine desired time to think, discuss, and write, and was not particularly interested in administrative leadership.

---

22 P. Monceaux, 'Saint Augustin et Saint Antoine. Contribution à l'histoire du monachism,' in *Miscellanea Agostiniana*, II (Rome, 1931): 74–75; quoted in Lancel, *Augustine*, 131.

23 Lancel, *Augustine*, 130.

24 *Ibid.*, 131.

Augustine was aware that persons looked up to him in Africa, and that some persons would certainly desire to bring him into leadership in this or that city. He had even considered forming a monastery in Africa.[25] But he had turned his back on anything like a prestigious academic career, for example, as a rhetor, and also wanted to avoid becoming a bishop or presbyter in a church.[26] He said: 'So much, though, did I dread the episcopate, that since I had already begun to acquire a reputation of some weight among the servants of God, I wouldn't go near a place where I knew there was no bishop.'[27] Hippo seemed a safe place to visit, as it did indeed have a bishop. But, while visiting a friend in Hippo, Augustine says, 'I was caught, I was made a priest, and by this grade I eventually came to the episcopate.'[28]

Indeed, in this visit to Hippo in 391, the congregation surrounds him and virtually 'forces' him to accept the role of priest. It seems that this was an act of passionate persuasion rather than force! The bishop of Hippo, Valerius, was older, and the church thought Augustine would be a wonderful successor. Augustine and Valerius served together until 395 or 396, at which time Augustine was ordained as priest, and eventually bishop, of Hippo.

It is perhaps surprising for us to learn that upon becoming priest at Hippo, Augustine felt an acute need for more theological study. Although he had already written a number of works, he believed he needed to learn even more. Augustine felt that he did not yet really know the Scriptures as well as he should. In a letter to bishop Valerius, Augustine speaks of his desire to study:

> I ought to examine carefully all the remedies of [God's] scriptures and, by praying and reading, work that He may grant my soul health suited for such dangerous tasks. I did not do this

---

25   Augustine, *Sermon* 355, 2.

26   *Ibid.*

27   *Ibid.*

28   *Ibid.*

before because I did not have the time. For I was ordained at the time when we were planning a period of retreat for gaining knowledge of the divine scriptures and wanted to arrange our affairs in order that we could have the leisure for this task.[29]

Augustine wanted time to read and write. But this was not to be—at least not in the sense of having a leisurely pace of life. Hippo had active Manichaean and Donatist communities; it was not simply a sleepy north African town. Augustine served as bishop until he died in 430. It is important to remember that during those 35 years he was a busy pastor. He performed weddings, counseled persons, advocated for his people with the civil authorities, and served as arbiter between persons in conflict. His literary output is astounding in itself, and all the more given that he spent almost the last half of his life in pastoral ministry.

A key part of Augustine's pastoral ministry was responding to doctrinal controversies and to requests for pastoral, biblical, and theological insight on various issues. It was during his years in Hippo that Augustine lived through, worked through, and wrote through three controversies that can help us grasp the significance of his perspective and his life:

1. The *Pelagian* controversy, centering on the nature of sin and grace
2. The *Donatist* controversy, centering on the nature of the church—and ultimately of the sacraments
3. The *Pagan* controversy, resulting in Augustine's *magnum opus*, *The City of God*—dealing with (virtually!) everything, and originating in pagan criticisms that the invasion of Rome by Alaric and the Visigoths (A.D. 410) was due to Rome's rejection of their traditional pagan gods and embrace of Christianity.

We will look at each of these three issues in some detail throughout the course of this book.

---

29 Augustine, *Letter* 21, 3.

Augustine died in 430, three years after *The City of God* was published. He was a busy pastor (i.e., a bishop, which means that he not only served a local population, but also a regional one). Serge Lancel has commented that Augustine was no 'egghead' theologian simply poring over texts and writing academic treatises. Instead, he wrote some of the most significant theological treatises ever written amidst the challenges of the busy life of a pastor. When he died he was still battling the Pelagians, in particular the feisty Julian of Eclanum (whom Lancel calls 'this hotheaded youngster who could have been his son').

For good or for ill—and I think largely for good—the Reformation tradition is in a great debt to Augustine, who laid much of the doctrinal edifice for the later Western tradition. This is especially so in his doctrine of grace, of which legacy the Reformational churches can rightly claim to be the true heir. Western theology has justifiably been called a long series of footnotes to Augustine. The Reformation churches differ from Augustine at points, as we will see. At the same time, Augustine is an important theologian in our tradition.

2

GOD

Augustine was a theologian in the truest sense: someone fascinated with, and intent on understanding, God. He was determined to know and love the God whom he had met. In this chapter we will explore several of Augustine's ideas about God.

The Quest for God[1]

For Augustine the 'quest' for God is something which—in one sense—is completed before it has begun. Augustine would

---

1   It is probably correct to see in Augustine the notion of our 'quest' for God as 'journey' or a 'trek,' and similar imagery. Protestants can affirm such imagery as biblical. Philippians 3:12-14 uses similar imagery: 'Not that I have already obtained this or am already perfect, but I press on to make it my own, because Christ Jesus has made me his own. Brothers, I do not consider that I have made it my own. But one thing I do: forgetting what lies behind and straining forward to what lies ahead, I press on toward the goal for the prize of the upward call of God in Christ Jesus.' Or Philippians 3:20: 'But our citizenship is in heaven, and from it we await a Savior, the Lord Jesus Christ.' The key principle for the Protestant reader is, in my opinion, to think about all biblical imagery in relationship to the whole canon of Scripture, and to try and ensure that no biblical imagery or metaphor takes on a life of its own that grows or mutates in unbiblical directions. As the reader will see throughout this volume, I believe it is critically important to link notions such as growth in Christ, progressive sanctification, and the transformation of the believer properly and explicitly to an Evangelical understanding of the gospel as

approve of Paul's quotation (perhaps from the Greek philosopher Epimenides of Crete) that: 'In him we live and move and have our being' (Acts 17:28).

That is to say: for Augustine, simply by *existing* we are already God's creatures living in God's world. We are dependent on Him even before we know it. Nonetheless, the 'quest'—in another sense—is a real one, is a process; it is a journey.

Although the following passage is speaking, it seems, of the *Christian*, one sees how Augustine can combine in one passage the two ideas that (1) we are already near Him (we are 'in' Him), but that we are nonetheless (2) still journeying 'toward' Him. Thus:

> But we by pressing on imitate Him who abides motionless; we follow Him who stands still, and by [1] walking in Him [note again: we are 'in Him'] we [2] move toward Him [we are still moving toward God], because for us He became a road or way in time by His humility, while being for us an eternal abode by His divinity.[2]

Wisdom and Knowledge

As we think about how Augustine thinks about our 'quest' for God, we should note: Augustine distinguished wisdom (*sapientia*) from knowledge (*scientia*). *Wisdom* is concerned with timeless, immutable, and eternal realities—the divine ideas, perhaps even God Himself; *knowledge* is concerned with temporal and mutable realities. Knowledge can and should serve the higher good of wisdom; that is, knowledge should be *oriented to* wisdom.

---

centered in the death, burial, resurrection, and appearances of Jesus. To put this candidly: we as believers are indeed 'pilgrims' on a journey to one day see God face-to-face (1 Cor. 13:12). But this journey must be plotted or understood in relation to the whole biblical storyline, and understood in proper relation to the doctrine of justification by faith alone, as well as the doctrine of being united with Christ by faith alone apart from works.

2 *On the Trinity* VII.5 (my enumeration and brackets).

Perhaps a chart will help:

Latin Term	English Term	Concerned with ...
scientia	'knowledge' or 'science'	Things human
sapientia	'wisdom'	Things divine

The notion that 'things human' should always and at all points be understood or make sense in relation to 'things divine' is precious, but is foreign to our current cultural milieu.

Faith and Reason

In the history of Christian thought, the best of Christian thinkers have—in their various ways—affirmed the existence and importance of questions of faith and reason. Augustine is no exception, and one way of making sense of our contemporary scene with respect to such questions of faith and reason is by asking how this or that thinker fundamentally differs from, or agrees with, some of Augustine's key principles.

Let's look first at the question of Augustine's understanding of faith and reason more generally. Augustine's position is rather sophisticated. At one point he writes:

> In certain matters, therefore, pertaining to the teaching of salvation, which we cannot yet grasp by reason, but which we will be able to at some point, faith precedes reason so that the heart may be purified in order that it may receive and sustain the light of the great reason, which is, of course, a demand of reason![3]

In other words, with at least some things—i.e., the teaching of salvation—faith precedes reason, at least at first, because the teaching of salvation appears not to be something immediately recognizable by our reason. So we begin with faith, and over

---

3   *Letter* 120, 1.3.

time our hearts are purified. As our hearts are purified, we are more and more able to reason—perhaps in a fuller and more robust sense. And this heightened/improved use of reason is indeed 'a demand of reason.'

Faith Seeking Understanding

As seen above, Augustine and a teacher who lived much later, St. Anselm (A.D. 1033–1109), are properly viewed as advocates of the perspective of 'faith seeking understanding.' This view is sometimes contrasted with the idea, often associated with Thomas Aquinas, that 'understanding seeks faith,' that is, that humans can reason their way to God.[4] What is the significance of Augustine's approach to the relationship of faith and reason?

One thing 'faith seeking understanding' does *not* mean is that there is some sort of hostility between faith and understanding (or reason). Also, it is not the case that 'faith' here can simply be first and foremost a non-cognitive (or non-thinking) reality. Rather, Augustine specifies that 'believing' is actually *always* preceded by 'thinking.' He writes:

> [E]verything which is believed should be believed after thought has preceded; although even belief itself is nothing else than to think with assent. For it is not everyone who thinks that believes, since many think in order that they may not believe; but everybody who believes, thinks—both thinks in believing, and believes in thinking.[5]

So, for Augustine, there is a type of *priority* to faith, in terms of faith's link to understanding. But it would be incorrect to surmise that faith is somehow *fundamentally* a non-thinking or non-cognitive reality.

But 'faith seeking understanding' also has another sense: Christian faith is a reality that is *inherently* and *inescapably* a

---

4   There may be some truth in this claim, but it is probably not completely fair to Thomas, either. More on that later.

5   *Predestination of the Saints* 5.

'seeking' reality. That is, true faith is something that seeks to (1) understand itself, and to (2) understand that which faith entails, or to understand what flows from faith. Thus, Christian faith—for Augustine—is something that is not satisfied to say simply, 'I have faith. That is all.' Rather, Christian faith is eager to understand what faith actually *is*, and to understand the myriad of things that faith points to, touches upon, influences, and entails.

We also see in Augustine a linking of (1) our spiritual state and (2) our ability to know or perceive things more truly. For instance, he says, '[The teachings of the Lord] are seen more clearly and known more perfectly by those better than we, even while they live on earth, and certainly by the good and pious after this life.'[6] Similarly, Augustine can speak of those who 'are able to gaze upon that Truth, which the pure mind beholds.'[7]

Additionally, Augustine is not unaware that our current and fallen state means that our present knowledge is not only partial and incomplete but also in various ways is caught up in the reality of fallenness.[8] As fallen persons we are liable to fail, and Augustine brings our liability to fail to bear on the life of the mind: 'But, owing to the liability of the human mind to fall into mistakes, this very pursuit of knowledge may be a snare to him unless he has a divine Master, whom he may obey without misgiving, and who may at the same time give him such help as to preserve his own freedom.'[9]

While we cannot linger long on this issue, I pause to make one point. It is on this question of the life of the mind that I think we can see what will later be a significant divide between Augustine and Thomas Aquinas. Briefly put: Augustine seems more explicit in fleshing out the effects of sin and human rebellion on

---

6   *On Free Choice* II.2.4–6.

7   *The Value of Believing*, 2.

8   *City of God* XIX.18.

9   *Ibid.*, XIX.14.

our knowing and thinking capacities. One might be able to find some quotations in Thomas where he says *something* like what Augustine is saying, but Thomas (and certainly much of the tradition that follows him) seems clearly to be more optimistic about man's knowing and thinking capacities, even in our post-fall state. This whole area of thinking and knowing is one where the line runs more clearly, in my opinion, from Augustine to the Reformation (especially the Reformed tradition) than from Augustine to Thomas (as well as to the Thomist tradition and to other strands of Roman Catholicism).

Who Is God, and How Should We Speak of God?

Much of Augustine's writing about God is inextricably bound up with the question: *How can I, a created, finite (and now fallen) creature approach, think, speak about, and know this God?*

Augustine is aware that one must be humble and careful when speaking about God. Augustine begins Book V of *The Trinity* with a disclaimer, admitting to the trepidation with which one ventures to speak of the divine nature or being: 'From now on I will be attempting to say things that cannot altogether be said as they are thought by a man—or at least as they are thought by me.'[10] Indeed, as Augustine continues:

> In any case, when we think about God the Trinity we are aware that our thoughts are quite inadequate to their object, and incapable of grasping Him as He is; even by men of the calibre of the apostle Paul He can only be seen, as it says, *like a puzzling reflection in a mirror* (1 Cor. 13:12).[11]

Augustine, like many Christian thinkers, wants to approach God in a way appropriate to who God is. Thus, he writes:

---

10   *The Trinity* V.1.

11   *Ibid.* 1 Cor 13:12 is a central passage for Augustine. Especially in *The Trinity*, Augustine asks: who is this God, and what is this God like, whom (according to 1 Cor. 13:12) I am going to one day see face to face?

[T]here is no effrontery in burning to know, out of faithful piety, the divine and inexpressible truth that is above us, provided the mind is fired by the grace of our creator and savior, and not inflated by arrogant confidence in its own powers.[12]

Augustine also contends that 'the total transcendence of the godhead quite surpasses the capacity of ordinary speech. God can be thought about more truly than He can be talked about, and He is more truly than He can be thought about.'[13] Augustine struggles to speak of God, but at the same time he cannot stop trying to speak of God.

The Triune God

One aspect of God in which Augustine displays supreme confidence, regardless of the limited nature of human speech, is God's triune nature. Augustine is thoroughly Trinitarian and is happy to accept the doctrine of God as Trinity on the basis of Scripture and tradition. Here is how he defines and explains the Trinity:

The purpose of all the Catholic commentators I have been able to read on the divine books of both testaments, who have written before me on the trinity which God is, has been to teach that according to the scriptures Father and Son and Holy Spirit in the inseparable equality of one substance present a divine unity; and therefore there are not three gods but one God; although indeed the Father has begotten the Son, and therefore He who is the Father is not the Son; and the Son is begotten by the Father, and therefore He who is the Son is not the Father; and the Holy Spirit is neither the Father nor the Son, but only the Spirit of the Father and of the Son, Himself coequal to the Father and the Son, and belonging to the threefold unity.[14]

---

12   *Ibid.*
13   *Ibid.*, VII.7
14   *Ibid.*, I.2.7.

Augustine wrestles at some length on making sense of the words
we (and Scripture) use to speak of God. He ultimately will speak
of 'substance' words (words which always denote the substance
of God) and 'accident' words (words which can be properly
used when speaking of God, but are not actually speaking of
the substance of God). While we speak of most things with
both 'substance' words and 'accident' words, when we speak of
God we are ultimately using simply 'substance' words. That is,
when we *truly* speak of God, we have to use substance words.
Why? Because whereas *we* (humans) sometimes possess certain
characteristics and sometimes do not (I am sometimes kind and
sometimes not), God possesses all of who He is all the time. Thus
Augustine writes, 'God is a substance (*substantia*), or perhaps a
better word would be being (*essentia*); at any rate what the Greeks
call *ousia* (*οὐσία*).'[15] While other things are also called 'beings'
(*essentiae*) or (*substantiae*), all such things (besides God) 'admit of
modifications (*accidentiae*).'[16]

Augustine summarizes his position at one point as follows:

> The chief point then that we must maintain is that whatever
> that supreme and divine majesty is called with reference to itself
> is said substance-wise; whatever it is called with reference to
> another is said not substance—but relationship-wise; and that
> such is the force of the expression 'of the same substance' in
> Father and Son and Holy Spirit, that whatever is said with
> reference to self about each of them is to be taken as adding up
> in all three to a singular and not to a plural.[17]

15   *Ibid.*, V.3.

16   *Ibid.* Roland Teske writes, 'Since there can be no accident in God, what seems to be
      said of God according to accident must be understood to be said of him according
      to substance, that is, must be understood to signify or designate the substance of
      God.' Roland J. Teske, 'Augustine's Use of "Substantia" in Speaking About God,'
      The Modern Schoolman LXII (March 1985): 149; cf. idem, 'Properties of God and
      the Predicaments in The Trinity V,' *The Modern Schoolman* LIX (1981): 1–19.

17   *Ibid.*, V.9.

Augustine's central point here is that Father and Son and Holy Spirit can be in some sense different without being of different substance. To demonstrate this, Augustine is laboring to show that 'Father' and 'Son' and 'Holy Spirit,' though different words, do not denote different substances. Why? Because the words/titles denote different *relationships* without denoting different substances. The difficulty that lurks in the background, and that Augustine will face below, is as follows: how can some words be spoken of God substance-wise and some not?

As Augustine writes, 'But for God it is the same thing to *be* as to be powerful or just or wise or anything else that can be said ... to signify His substance.'[18] Augustine also concludes that it is necessary that all substance words be applicable to both Father and Son, because 'the Son is in no way equal to the Father, if He is found in any way that has to do with signifying His substance to be unequal.'[19]

Augustine then includes the Holy Spirit in his discussion and contends that substance words must be applicable to the Holy Spirit as well. He writes, 'But just as it [i.e. the Holy Spirit] is substance together with the Father and the Son, so is it great together and good together and holy together with them and whatever else is said with reference to self, because with God it is not a different thing to be, and to be great or good, etc.'[20] The equality of the Holy Spirit with the other members of the Trinity is ultimately grounded in the simplicity of God: 'The Holy Spirit is equal too, and if equal, equal in every respect, on account of the total simplicity which belongs to that substance.'[21]

Augustine confidently affirms the co-equality and full deity of the three persons of the Trinity:

---

18   *Ibid.*, VI.6, emphasis mine.

19   *Ibid.*

20   *Ibid.*, VI.7.

21   *Ibid.*

[W]e have demonstrated as briefly as we could the equality of the triad and its one identical substance. So whatever may be the solution of this question, which we have put off for more searching examination, there is nothing now to prevent us from acknowledging the supreme equality of Father, Son, and Holy Spirit.[22]

Additionally, Augustine and the tradition that follows him are credited with the Latin maxim: *opera trinitatis ad extra sunt indivisa* ('the external works of the Trinity are undivided'). This isn't an argument that today's Christians make every day, so, what does it mean? Essentially, Augustine is stating that all three persons of the Godhead are involved in all that God does 'outside' Himself—i.e., creation, redemption, and governance/providence of the world. Perhaps the clearest example of this doctrine can be found in one of Augustine's letters to Nebridius:

For the Catholic faith teaches and believes that this Trinity is so inseparable—and a few holy and blessed men also understand this—that whatever this Trinity does must be thought to be done at the same time by the Father and by the Son and by the Holy Spirit. The Father does not do anything that the Son and the Holy Spirit do not do, nor does the Son do anything that the Father and the Holy Spirit do not do, nor does the Holy Spirit do anything that the Father and the Son do not do.[23]

This is a very important insight, one which has been rightfully affirmed throughout the centuries by traditional Christians. It helps to secure or support the notion that the persons of the Godhead always act in complete accord, and to counteract tritheism, or the idea that there are three separate gods.

---

22   Ibid., VI.10.
23   *Letter 11 (Augustine to Nebridius)*, 2. Cf. *A Handbook on Faith, Hope, and Love* 12.38: 'The operations of the Trinity are inseparable' (*opera trinitatis ad extra sunt indivisa*).

Augustine, The Trinity, and Analogies

When someone takes a course on the Trinity, it is not uncommon to get to the development of the doctrine of the Trinity and to be told something like: 'Well, Augustine's approach was to go into the inner psyche or aspect of man, and to find analogies for the Trinity, sometimes called "psychological analogies."' If the teacher is a bit disaffected with Augustine, there might be an additional comment to the effect that 'Augustine, because he went into the human psyche to discover analogies for the Trinity, severed the Triune God from the world—from the realms of creation and redemption.' Perhaps I exaggerate a bit here, but not by much.

In fact, Augustine is doing something quite fascinating when he writes on the Trinity, and this does indeed include Augustine reflecting on this or that analogy. But what, exactly, is Augustine doing? Augustine begins his work *The Trinity* with an affirmation of the Trinity. Scripture teaches it, it is the tradition of the Christian church, and Augustine firmly believes in it. There is a clear polemical tone, and Augustine is on the 'watch against the sophistries of those who scorn the starting-point of faith, and allow themselves to be deceived through an unseasonable and misguided love of reason.'[24]

Augustine then turns to 1 Corinthians 13:12: 'For now we see in a mirror dimly, but then face to face. Now I know in part; then I shall know fully, even as I have been fully known.' Augustine asks: what is this God going to be like that I will one day see face to face? After working through some thorny issues (such as what to make of the 'missions' or theophanies in the Old Testament, and how do we speak properly of God), he 'turns inward.' That is, he argues that man is made in the image of God, and if the mind of man is essentially the 'seat' of the image of God in man (Augustine's supposition), then one should be able to make this 'inward' turn and explore and discover—perhaps!—something of

24 *The Trinity* I.1.

a 'trace' or 'vestige' of the Trinity in man. And this turn inward
leads to the discussion of various 'psychological analogies.'

This is all true, but what is sometimes missed is that many
of these analogies are trotted out, explored, and ultimately set
aside as not particularly helpful. Thus, Augustine can speak of
'memory, understanding, and will';[25] 'lover, being loved, and
love'[26]; 'the mind, its love, and its knowledge';[27] 'memory, sight,
and love'[28]. There are a number of other similar analogies.

At two points in *The Trinity*, Augustine will linger at length
on the incarnation and the atoning death of Christ.[29] Why is
Augustine doing this in a book on the Trinity? What Augustine
argues is the following. The Trinity is true because it is clearly
taught in Scripture, and the church has also historically affirmed
the doctrine of the Trinity. And the Christian will one day see
this Triune God face to face. But in order to be in the presence
of God, and see God face to face, we must be changed and
transformed by the blood of Christ. If other philosophies or
theologies (he has the Neoplatonists in mind, it seems clear) can
posit that we get back to God essentially by our own efforts,
Augustine is arguing that the human creature can only 'return'
to God, or be in God's presence because God—in the form of
the Son—has come down to us in the Incarnation, and has died
for us in His atoning death. Since the face-to-face vision is at
least in part *intellectual*, the blood of Christ must cleanse our
minds if we are going to see God.

As one reads *The Trinity*, it is as if one is watching Augustine
slowly work through one analogy after another, with Augustine
each time setting this or that analogy aside because of its
inadequacies. But toward the end of *The Trinity*, Augustine

---

25   *Ibid.*, IV.30; X:17-19; XIV: 8, 10.

26   *Ibid.*, VIII:14; IX:2.

27   *Ibid.*, IX:4, 6, 7, 8, 15, 18.

28   *Ibid.*, XIV: 11; XV:39.

29   This is seen in books IV and XIII of *The Trinity*.

returns to a key analogy from Book X: the mind remembering, understanding, and willing (or loving) itself. But something else is happening as well. As Augustine tries to properly understand and articulate what *God the Trinity* is like, he is also (somewhat subtly) leading the reader to confront the following: *how can the image of God in man be properly restored so that the face-to-face vision of God is possible?* For Augustine it is not simply the possession of a mental faculty that allows the image of God to be realized (i.e., not just having a mind that is somehow 'trinitarian' in some sense). Rather, it is the mind *engaged in certain activities* that allows the image of God to be realized.

It appears that Augustine has arrived at his goal: the image of God is realized, and we get the best glimpse of the Trinity, when we land upon the notion of the mind remembering, understanding, and loving itself. Augustine writes: 'Here we are then with the mind remembering itself, understanding itself, loving itself. If we see this we see a trinity, not yet God of course, but already the image of God.'[30] One of the key reasons Augustine lands here is because the mind—like God—is co-eternal with its remembering, understanding, and loving itself. That is, as soon as the mind came to be, we can say it was engaged in remembering, understanding, and loving itself.

Then, in a fascinating twist, Augustine advances the argument. The best analogy is *not* the mind remembering, understanding, and loving *itself*, but the mind remembering, understanding, and loving *God*.[31] Indeed: 'This trinity of the mind is not really the image of God because the mind remembers and understands and loves itself, but because it is also able to remember and understand and love him by whom it was made. And when it does this it becomes wise. If it does not do it, then even though it remembers and understands and loves itself, it is foolish.'[32] Here

---

30   *Ibid.*, XIV.11.

31   *Ibid.*, XIV.15.

32   *Ibid.*

we are getting to the heart of the matter: 'Let it then remember its God to whose image it was made, and understand and love Him. To put it in a word, let it worship the uncreated God, by whom it was created with a capacity for Him and able to share in Him.'[33]

And at the end of Book XIV, Augustine turns explicitly to the fact that the image is somewhat defaced, and is need of reconstruction and reforming and renovation. And now we see more fully why Augustine's 'excurses' on the atonement in Books IV and XIII were *central* and not *peripheral* to the argument. We need to be reformed and renovated if the image is going to be fully restored in us and if we are going to one day truly see God face-to-face—as Paul speaks about in 1 Corinthians 13:12.

Classical Theism

The theological tradition that, generally speaking, came to dominate in the historic Christian church, whether Protestant, Roman Catholic, or Eastern Orthodox, is sometimes referred to as 'classical theism.' Augustine is one of the architects of classical theism. Though this term covers much more than can be discussed here, we will briefly review Augustine's perspective on divine simplicity, divine immutability, God and time, and God and knowledge.

Divine Simplicity

Historically, when Christian theologians have spoken of divine simplicity, they have essentially meant that God is not a compound being. That is, He is not a bunch of different 'things' brought together to make one 'thing.' The basic logic is quite simple: If God *is* a compound of different things or 'stuff,' then there is something (the various things or various 'stuff') which precedes God. But how could *that* be? God would have to be there to create the things or 'stuff' in the first place. So, we end

---

up with: surely God is the first reality that exists. In short, there are simply two realms of reality: Creator and created. In the beginning, there was simply God. And He Himself was (and is) 'simple'—a being who is not made up of other things or stuff.[34]

Augustine describes the simplicity of God this way: 'There is, accordingly, a good which is alone simple, and therefore alone unchangeable, and this is God. By this good have all others been created, but not simple, and therefore not unchangeable.'[35] Augustine goes on to say:

> And this Trinity is one God; and none the less simple because a Trinity. For we do not say that the nature of the good is simple, because the Father alone possesses it, or the Son alone, or the Holy Ghost alone; nor do we say, with the Sabellian heretics, that it is only nominally a Trinity, and has no real distinction of persons; but we say it is simple, because it is what it has, with the exception of the relation of the persons to one another. For, in regard to this relation, it is true that the Father has a Son, and yet is not Himself the Son, and the Son has a Father, and is not Himself the Father. But as regards Himself, irrespective of relation to the other, each is what He has; thus, He is in Himself living, for He has life, and is Himself the Life which He has.[36]

Divine Immutability

Augustine clearly affirms the doctrine of divine immutability, 'the unchangeable substance of God.'[37] Indeed, 'there is no unchangeable good but the one, true, blessed God; that the things which He made are indeed good because from Him, yet mutable

---

34   I am simply summarizing here. This is a big issue worthy of some serious reflection and reading.

35   *City of God* XI.10.

36   *Ibid.* XI.10.

37   *Ibid.* XI.2.

because made not out of Him, but out of nothing.'[38] Likewise, 'For since God is the supreme existence, that is to say, supremely is, and is therefore unchangeable, the things that He made He empowered to be, but not to be supremely like Himself.'[39]

The creation of the world in no way impinges upon God's sovereignty and immutability. Augustine writes: 'For this is a depth indeed, that God always has been, and that man, whom He had never made before, He willed to make in time, and this without changing His design and will.'[40]

The fact that God exhibits anger does not impinge upon His immutability. Augustine writes, 'The anger of God is not a disturbing emotion of His mind, but a judgment by which punishment is inflicted upon sin. His thought and reconsideration also are the unchangeable reason which changes things; for He does not, like man, repent of anything He has done, because in all matters His decision is as inflexible as His prescience is certain.'[41]

God and Time

Augustine repeatedly and consistently teaches that God is eternal and is Lord over time. Indeed, time itself is a created reality. Augustine writes: 'For, though Himself eternal, and without beginning, yet He caused time to have a beginning; and man, whom He had not previously made, He made in time, not from a new and sudden resolution, but by His unchangeable and eternal design.'[42] Indeed: 'God always has been, and that man, whom He had never made before, He willed to make in time, and this without changing His design and will.'[43]

---

38   Ibid. XII.1.

39   Ibid., XII.2.

40   Ibid., XII.14.

41   Ibid., XV.25.

42   Ibid., XII.14.

43   Ibid.

In *Confessions* Augustine takes up the question, 'What was God doing before He created the world?' Augustine does not think that the question is a very good one. His answer: 'Before God made heaven and earth, He was not doing anything; for if He was doing or making something, what else would He be doing but creating? And no creature was made before any creature was made. I wish I could know everything that I desire to know to my own profit with the same certainty with which I know that.'[44]

God and Knowledge

To speak of Augustine's understanding of God and knowledge is of course to be still in the world of divine timelessness. Thus, when Augustine quotes from Genesis, 'And God saw that it was good,' he then writes: 'For certainly God did not in the actual achievement of the work first learn that it was good, but, on the contrary, nothing would have been made had it not been first known by Him.'[45] For God does not know like we know:

> For not in our fashion does He look forward to what is future, nor at what is present, nor back upon what is past; but in a manner quite different and far and profoundly remote from our way of thinking. For He does not pass from this to that by transition of thought, but beholds all things with absolute unchangeableness; so that of those things which emerge in time, the future, indeed, are not yet, and the present are now, and the past no longer are; but all of these are by Him comprehended in His stable and eternal presence.[46]

And Augustine goes on to delineate how God's knowledge differs from ours, and how this vast knowledge implies no change in God:

---

44   *Ibid.*, XI.12.14.

45   *Ibid.*, XI.21.

46   *Ibid.*

Neither does He see in one fashion by the eye, in another by the mind, for He is not composed of mind and body; nor does His present knowledge differ from that which it ever was or shall be, for those variations of time, past, present, and future, though they alter our knowledge, do not affect His, 'with whom is no variableness, neither shadow of turning.' Neither is there any growth from thought to thought in the conceptions of Him in whose spiritual vision all things which He knows are at once embraced. For as without any movement that time can measure, He Himself moves all temporal things, so He knows all times with a knowledge that time cannot measure.[47]

Augustine, of course, does not see God as being 'in' time. Augustine writes that it would be a mighty miracle indeed if God were to know all things in the way that a human mind knows. But God's knowledge of all things is even greater, since God *does* know all things but does *not* know like we humans know:

But far be it from us to suppose that you, the creator of the universe, creator of souls and bodies, know all things future and past in this fashion! Perish the thought! Far, far more wonderful is your mode of knowing, and far more mysterious. When a person is singing words well known to him, or listening to a familiar song, his senses are strained between anticipating sounds still to come and remembering those sung already; but with you it is quite otherwise. Nothing can happen to you in your unchangeable eternity, you who are truly the eternal creator of all minds. As you knew heaven and earth in the beginning, without the slightest modification in your knowledge, so too you made heaven and earth in the beginning without any distension in your activity.[48]

---

47 *Ibid.*

48 *Ibid.*, XI.31.41. 'Distension' is not a word that we use a lot today. It essentially means 'to stretch out' or 'to expand.' So, in this context, Augustine is saying that God can know all things without 'stretching' or 'expanding' in His knowledge. When you or I know, by contrast, our minds do 'stretch' or 'expand.' Interestingly, cognitive research confirms Augustine's wording here: when you or I engage in serious, sustained study, there is an actual change in our brain. This is not the case with God!

Augustine helped lay the foundation for the church's thinking about who God is and how we can properly speak of God. God can be known and spoken about—even in human words!—but never in a way that exhausts who God is. God Himself truly 'knows,' but not as creatures know. The words of Scripture speak truly, but not exhaustively, of God. We can speak of God using different attributes—good, holy, just, gracious, etc., but God is ultimately one, and is not a combination of parts. This God is triune, and the three persons are all God, but are somehow three different persons. This God who is immutable also creates, and also enters into the time and space in the incarnation, as we will see in the following chapters.

3

CREATION AND PROVIDENCE

Augustine, Creation, and Genesis
Having once been a Manichee, but now a Christian, it is no surprise that Augustine spent significant time thinking and writing on the nature of creation in general and on the book of Genesis in particular. In fact, Augustine wrote several works on Genesis, including *On the Literal Interpretation of Genesis* (c. 401–415); *Unfinished Literal Commentary on Genesis* (c. 393/394; two paragraphs added in 427); and *On Genesis, against the Manichees* (c. 389). Augustine also comments on creation and/or Genesis throughout his writings, as in sections of *The City of God* (413–427) and *Confessions* (c. 397–401).

Augustine on Interpreting Genesis
Augustine wrestled at great lengths in attempting to understand the book of Genesis. Augustine advocates humility for the interpreter: 'Only avoid asserting anything rashly, and something you don't know as if you did; and remember that you are just a human being investigating the works to the extent that you are permitted to do so.'[1] In the opening section of his *Unfinished Literal Commentary on Genesis*, Augustine makes a number of

---

1   *Unfinished Literal Commentary on Genesis*, IX.30.

interpretative suggestions. For instance, since we are dealing with the 'obscure mysteries of the natural order,' one should ask questions (of the Bible) rather than make affirmations. But this does not allow one never to believe or affirm anything positive about what the Scriptures mean. Rather, one should be guided by the 'bounds of Catholic faith.' In short, Augustine's emphasis on asking questions does not mean approaching Genesis with simply one long series of questions, but rather proceeding in a spirit of inquiry and humility. It also does not mean ranging into speculative interpretations unmoored to the essential truths of historic ('Catholic') Christianity.[2]

In summarizing how to approach Genesis, in his unfinished commentary on Genesis, Augustine describes four kinds of meaning one might find in Scripture. These are not unique to him, but reflect a pattern of interpretation common within the ancient church:

1. *Historical* (the historical, literal, or plain sense: 'when things done by God or man are recounted.')
2. *Allegorical* (the allegorical or figurative sense: 'when they are understood figuratively.')
3. *Analogical* (the analogical or 'whole Bible' sense: 'when the harmony of the old and new covenants is being demonstrated.')
4. *Aetiological* (the sense having to do with causes: 'when the causes of things that have been said and done are presented.')[3]

Augustine quite happily affirms the importance, even primacy, of the historical or literal sense of Scripture. Augustine takes the genealogies of Scriptures as factual, believes in the long lives of the pre-flood persons of the Old Testament, and can even suggest how long man has been on the earth. Thus, in *The City of*

---

2   *Ibid.*, I.1.

3   *Ibid.*, I.2.

God (12.11) Augustine reasons: 'On the basis of Sacred Scripture, however, we calculate that not even six thousand years have passed since the origin of mankind.' Along these lines, Augustine clearly affirms a real, or 'literal,' Adam. In speaking of the early chapters of Genesis, Augustine writes: 'All these things stood for something other than what they were, but all the same they were themselves bodily entities. And when the narrator mentioned them, he was not employing figurative language, but giving an explicit account of things which had a forward reference that was figurative.'[4] Augustine did read Scripture figuratively, often more so than we today would be comfortable with. But he did so while also taking seriously the literal reference of the text.

The Goodness and Order of Creation

For Augustine, God created a completely good world. At one point he writes: 'We know, therefore, that we should attribute to the creator, not defects, but natures, but one who wants to resist Mani must say where the defects come from.'[5] Though explaining the world's 'defects' is sometimes necessary in an apologetical context, Augustine maintains that a focus on the goodness of creation is desirable.

Creation is not only good, but ordered and hierarchical. Augustine writes: 'With respect to their own nature ... the

---

4   *Ibid.*, VIII.4.8.

5   *Against Julian, an Unfinished Book* IV.123. This can be a bit tricky to our contemporary ears. In this volume Augustine has just quoted Ephesians 2:3, where Paul speaks of sinners being 'by nature, objects of wrath.' In his polemic against Julian and the Pelagians, as well as the Manichees in this particular passage, Augustine is trying to argue that nothing whatsoever is sinful or evil by nature. This is because God creates all things. He creates 'natures.' He does not create 'defects.' The Christian must account for how sin, evil, or 'defects' come along. But all that was originally created (i.e., all 'nature' things) were by nature good. Thus, with Ephesians 2:3: All persons are created good and not as objects of wrath. Due to the sin, persons become objects of wrath. But persons are not created as such. Our 'nature'—in being created—is not such that we are objects of wrath. We become objects of wrath.

creatures are glorifying to their Artificer.'[6] Augustine can also say, 'All natures, then, inasmuch as they are, and have therefore a rank and species of their own, and a kind of internal harmony, are certainly good. And when they are in the places assigned to them by the order of their nature, they preserve such being as they have received.'[7]

Augustine also argues for a notion of 'seminal causes.' Augustine's argument is that, when God created the world, He both created actual 'stuff'—animals, vegetation, etc., but also created seminal causes by which (over time) 'new' things would come forth. Thus, at some point *after* the original creation, we really do see 'new' creatures, 'new' vegetable life, and the like. But when animals reproduce, or when the seeds of a plant lead to the existence of a new plant, there is no *autonomous* creating going on. Rather, God is still the *ultimate* creator, because within humans—or within other living things—exist these seeds *created by God*, and only through these seeds does new life come into being.[8]

Creatio Ex Nihilo and the Nature of Time

For Augustine, God is a changeless and timeless being who creates out of nothing. Indeed, the notion of creation out of nothing allows Augustine to affirm that God truly is unchangeable. For if God creates somehow *out of* Himself, or *from* Himself, it is hard to see how God could remain unchangeable. It is at this very point that Augustine differs from Plotinus and the Neo-Platonists. Whereas Plotinus contends that creation is ultimately a necessity, Augustine attributes the reality and act of creation solely to the will of God. For Augustine God creates because

---

6   *The City of God* XII.4.

7   *Ibid.*, XII.5.

8   *The Trinity* III.13. Augustine speaks of rationes seminales or causales in his work, *On the Literal Interpretation of Genesis* V and VI.

He *wants* to, and out of *goodness*, not because the creative act is somehow a necessity.[9]

Augustine argues that 'the world was made, not in time, but simultaneously with time.'[10] Indeed, 'Since then, God, in whose eternity is no change at all, is the Creator and Ordainer of time, I do not see how He can be said to have created the world after spaces of time had elapsed, unless it be said that prior to the world there was some creature by whose movement time could pass.'[11]

'Heavens and Earth'

Turning to Genesis 1–'In the beginning God created the heavens and the earth,' Augustine pictures the *heavens* as a particularly 'high' level of creation, and the 'earth' as an especially 'low' level of creation. For Augustine the original 'earth' (of 'heavens and earth') is a 'lower' reality, but it does in fact exist. If it *were* in fact 'nothingness,' it would cease to exist. Augustine writes: 'The primal abyss was almost nothingness, for it was still totally without form, although it did exist, since it had the capacity to receive form.'[12] Likewise, Augustine can speak of this earth as 'the formless matter, invisible, unorganized and deeper than the deepest darkness.'[13] And God then takes this original 'earth' and works to form it more and more into what it should be.

Creation Days and the Creation Week

Concerning the days of the creation week, Augustine writes: 'What kind of days these were it is extremely difficult, or perhaps impossible for us to conceive, and how much more to

---

9   *Explanations of the Psalms* CXXXIV.10

10   *City of God* XI.6.

11   *Ibid.*, XI.6.

12   *Ibid.*, XII.8.8.

13   *Ibid.*, XII.8.8.

say!'[14] Augustine reads Sirach 18:1 to teach that God creates everything all at once. Hence, there is a puzzle: why does Genesis then portray creation as taking place over six days? Unlike some moderns, he is not trying to account for an older earth scenario, nor is he trying to square Genesis with evolutionary scenarios. He has his own questions which interest him. At the principled or philosophical level, Augustine's question is not, 'How do I square an ancient earth with seven creation days?' but rather, 'Why would the God of the Bible need or take *any* time to create? Why not simply create it all in an instant?' Augustine is also cautious about the nature of light during the first three days of creation: 'But what kind of light that was, and by what periodic movement it made evening and morning, is beyond the reach of our senses; neither can we understand how it was, and yet must unhesitatingly believe it.'[15]

Creation and the Will of God

For Augustine, creation clearly reveals that it is a created reality: 'The world itself, by its well-ordered changes and movements, and by the fair appearance of all visible things, bears a testimony of its own, both that it has been created, and also that it could not have been created save by God, whose greatness and beauty are unutterable and invisible.'[16]

Thus, on Augustine's own terms, God creates because He *wills* to do so, but He *wills* to do what is loving and good. That is, God creates out of His goodness. This point is most clearly illustrated from Augustine's chapter on creation in book thirteen of the *Confessions*. He affirms, 'Your creation has its being from the fullness of your goodness,'[17] and 'you made [creation] not because you needed it, but from the fullness of your goodness,

14   *Ibid.*, XI.6.

15   *Ibid.*, XI.7.

16   *Ibid.*, XI.4.

17   *Ibid.*, XIII.2.2.

imposing control and converting it to receive form—but not as if the result brought you fulfillment of delight.'[18]

Why does this matter? Sometimes Augustine (and others) can be criticized or dismissed by making creation seem almost arbitrary or disconnected from other theological realities—like redemption. The argument goes as follows: in Augustine, God creates *simply* out of brute will, and this creative act is not organically or really linked to the rest of the history of redemption (e.g., to redemption itself). I think this misses the mark. First, since Augustine affirms that God is all of His attributes at once (one way of speaking about the 'simplicity' of God), His *will* is always linked to His *goodness*. Hence, it really does not make sense to divorce (1) the idea that God creates because He *wills* to do so from (2) the truth that God is fundamentally *good*. That is: there is no 'brute' will in God because God always wills in relationship to His goodness. Second, when one reads Augustine it seems clear that He often links (1) creation to (2) redemption.[19]

What About Evil?

Perhaps one of Augustine's key contributions to Western (particularly Western and Christian) understandings of reality and of metaphysics is his reflections on the nature of evil. Let us turn to Augustine's notion of evil in general, and the notion of *privatio boni* in particular.

Evil as *Privatio Boni*

For Augustine evil is ultimately not a positive force in itself, but merely a privation of good, or *privatio boni*. He notes in one of his anti-Pelagian writings:

---

18 *Ibid.*, XIII.3.4.

19 I have tried to argue this at some length in my *Colin Gunton and the Failure of Augustine: The Theology of Colin Gunton in Light of Augustine* (Eugene, OR: Wipf and Stock, 2011).

Those things which we call evil are either the defects of good things, which cannot exist anywhere by themselves outside of good things, or they are the punishments of sins, which arise from the beauty of justice.... [E]vil is only a privation of good. Thus it never exists except in some good thing, which is not supremely good, for something supremely good, such as God, lasts without corruption or change. Still, evil exists only in something good, because it does harm only by diminishing what is good. Thus good things can exist without evil, as God himself and any loftier beings of heaven, but evils cannot exist without something good.[20]

Augustine likewise confirms: '[E]vil has no positive nature; but the loss of good has received the name "evil."'[21] And thus, opposition to God is not by *nature* but by *vice*. As Augustine writes: 'In Scripture they are called God's enemies who oppose His rule, not by nature, but by vice.... It is not nature, therefore, but vice, which is contrary to God.'[22]

Besides speaking of evil as the privation of good (which Augustine consistently does), Augustine can also speak of how God *uses* evil, or sin, for good. We might call this a type of utilitarian argument. For instance, Augustine says:

But evils are so thoroughly overcome by good, that though they are permitted to exist, for the sake of demonstrating how the most righteous foresight of God can make a good use even of them, yet good can exist without evil, as in the true and supreme God Himself ... but evil cannot exist without good, because the natures in which evil exists, in so far as they are natures, are good.[23]

Behind Augustine's understanding of evil as a *privatio boni* is an explicitly Christian attempt to avoid his former errors of

---

20   *Answer to an Enemy of the Law and the Prophets* I.5.7.

21   *The City of God* XI.9.

22   Ibid., XII.3.

23   Ibid., XIV.11.

Manichaeism, which posited a dualism of good and evil, both in eternity and in the very structure of reality. Having once embraced such a dualism, Augustine now rejected his former way of thinking. So instead, Augustine was led to see *existence* as *fundamentally* a good thing. Thus, Augustine states, 'Everything that exists is good, then; and so evil, the source of which I was seeking, cannot be a substance, because if it were, it would be good.'[24] That is, all existence, every substance, is fundamentally good. Thus, if things 'are deprived of all good, they will be simply non-existent; and so it follows that as long as they do exist, they are good.'[25]

God and Providence

That God sovereignly rules over all of the created order is manifestly clear in Augustine's writings. He writes, 'God can never be believed to have left the kingdoms of men, their dominations and servitudes, outside of the laws of His providence.'[26] To deny such providence is indeed foolish: 'For he who denies that all things, which either angels or men can give us, are in the hand of the one Almighty, is a madman.'[27] And God's providence is exhaustive: 'You see, dearly beloved, there is nothing that escapes providence.'[28]

Even the Scriptures themselves are hard to understand and take great work to interpret—and this too is due to the providence of God: 'This is all due, I have no doubt at all, to divine providence, in order to break in pride with hard labor, and to save the intelligence from boredom, since it readily forms a low opinion of things that are too easy to work out.'[29]

---

24   *Ibid.*, VII.12.18.

25   *Ibid.*

26   *Ibid.*, V.11.

27   *Ibid.*, X.14.

28   Sermon 8, *On the Plagues of Egypt and the Ten Commandments of the Law* 10.

29   *On Christian Doctrine* II.6.7.

The Scriptures, which contain the Law pointing to the Gospel, have been arranged just the way they are according to divine providence:

> The fulfillment and the end of the law and of all the divine scriptures is love (Rom. 13:8; 1 Tim. 1:5); love of the thing which is to be enjoyed, and of the thing which is able to enjoy that thing together with us, because there is no need for a commandment that we should love ourselves. So in order that we might know how to do this and be able to, the whole ordering of time was arranged by divine providence for our salvation.[30]

Additionally, Judas' betrayal of Jesus, which is portrayed in the New Testament, was determined by God (Luke 22:21–22). Augustine describes God's providential action as follows:

> [Jesus Christ] has used His brother's [i.e., Judas'] willful self-destruction, that is the despicable crime of His betrayer, to serve the dispensation of His own mercy and providence, so that what Judas did with perverse intention to bring about the death of one individual person, Christ Jesus was able by His guiding providence to direct for the salvation of all men and women.[31]

For Augustine the rejection of providence is ultimately a spiritual issue, and evidence of unbelief: 'Whoever entertains doubts about God's providence in any particular does not confess to God with a whole heart.'[32] Augustine reveals a stunning insight concerning man, his sin, and one's understanding of providence. Augustine asserts that a mark of the person who is sinking into sin is that they deny divine providence; at least they deny that providence extends to them! He writes:

---

30   *Ibid.*, I.35.39.

31   *Exposition of Psalm 7* (verse 1).

32   *Exposition of Psalm 9* (verse 2).

Scripture warns, 'A person devoid of reverence goes deep into sin and is defiant' (Prov. 18:3). The ones who go down into the lake of the dead are those who lose even the will to confess. Against such a fate the psalmist prays, 'Do not let the pit close its mouth over me' (Ps. 68:16).[33] A depth like this is often called a lake in scripture. When a sinner has plumbed such depths, he is defiant. In what sense? He no longer believes in any divine providence; or, if he does believe in it, he does not think it extends to himself.[34]

Gods' Providence Over Evil

Christian theologians have habitually affirmed God's providential rule over the created order, and this belief simply seems to be demanded of the person who takes the Bible seriously. At the same time, Christian thinkers often want to nuance how one speaks of (1) God's sovereign rule over good and (2) God's sovereign rule over sin and/or evil. Augustine is no exception. Thus, he can write:

> It is amazing and yet true that little ones are kindled with intense and hopeful enthusiasm to live upright lives, by the negative example of sinners. As part of the same mystery it happens that even heresies are allowed to exist, not because heretics themselves intend it so but because divine providence brings this result from their sins. It is providence which both makes and orders the light, but does no more than order the darkness.[35]

Notice the distinction: (1) providence *makes* and *orders* the light, but (2) providence 'no more than' *orders* the darkness. Augustine appears to want to affirm God's providence over *all* things, but

---

33   The enumeration of the Septuagint (LXX; the Greek Bible of the Old Testament) would match Psalm 69:15 in our English translations.

34   *Exposition of Psalm* 42.13.

35   *Exposition of Psalm* 9.20.

to make an understandable distinction between how God rules over good and evil.

We may not know why things happen, but Augustine encourages Christians to trust in the goodness of God, and that He rules justly:

> Whatever happens here that is not to our liking, recognize that it happens only in accordance with God's will, by His providence, as part of His design, by His permission, and in conformity with His laws. Even if we do not understand why something happens, let us ascribe it to his providence, certain that it does not happen without a good reason, and then we do not blaspheme.[36]

Augustine teaches that God is sovereign over all things, including evil and sin. Like virtually every significant theologian, he desires to state this carefully and thoughtfully. Augustine makes a distinction between God *creating* and God *ruling*. He writes:

> But God, as He is the supremely good *Creator* of good natures, so is He of evil wills the most just *Ruler*; so that, while they make an ill use of good natures, He makes a good use even of evil wills. Accordingly, He caused the devil (good by God's creation, wicked by his own will) to be cast down from his high position, and to become the mockery of His angels—that is, He caused his temptations to benefit those whom he wishes to injure by them.[37]

God certainly knew that in creating the world, a portion of the created order would turn against Him. But God determined to create the world nonetheless:

> It is He who, when He foreknew that certain angels would in their pride desire to suffice for their own blessedness, and would forsake their great good, did not deprive them of this power, deeming it to be more befitting His power and goodness

---

36   *Exposition of Psalm* 148.12 (commenting on verse 8).

37   *City of God*, XI.17. Emphasis mine.

to bring good out of evil than to prevent the evil from coming into existence.[38]

Toward the end of *The City of God*, Augustine speaks of God's willing of those things which He—as God—would not and does not do: 'According to this will which God works in men, He is said also to will what He Himself does not will, but causes His people to will; as He is said to know what He has caused those to know who were ignorant of it.... He wills many things which He does not perform.'[39]

---

38   *Ibid.*, XXII.1.
39   *Ibid.*, XX.2.

4

MAN AS CREATED, MAN AS FALLEN

One of the most fundamental questions anyone faces is: who am I? What does it mean to be human? Augustine pondered this question at great length. We are created—and hence majestic beings in some sense. We are also now tragically fallen. And as *still* created, and *still* existing (i.e., fallen man has not disappeared from the planet), we are still in some sense 'good.' These are dense issues indeed, but important to unpack, because they affect how we see ourselves as well as the work of God on our behalf.

Man as Created

Augustine is clear that each person is a created being, even if (obviously) each person is biologically brought into being by the union of the mother and father. Augustine writes: 'For even parents cannot make a human being; rather, God makes one by means of the parents.'[1] Augustine is forthright in speaking of Divine Providence in the creation of new persons, even if sin is at times involved in conception:

> I do not deny that 'the hand of divine providence is present in the genital organs of sinners.' After all, [the hand of God]

---

1   *Answer to Julian* III.18.34.

reaches from one end to another and arranges all things with
might and gentleness, and nothing defiled touches it. For this
reason it does what it wants with the unclean and infected,
while itself remaining clean and uninfected.[2]

Augustine affirms that God created the first man, and that man
was meant to be 'a mean between the angelic and bestial.'[3] The
first man was created and placed in the garden, given all he
needed, and called to obey. Augustine writes that if man had

... remained in subjection to his Creator as his rightful Lord,
and piously kept His commandments, he should pass into the
company of the angels, and obtain, without the intervention
of death, a blessed and endless immortality; but if he offended
the Lord his God by a proud and disobedient use of his free
will, he should become subject to death, and live as the beasts
do—the slave of appetite, and doomed to eternal punishment
after death.[4]

Created Man as Good?

One of the challenging issues in Christian history has been the
question of Adam and his sin, including *why* he sinned or *what
led* him to sin. There is a certain temptation, when speaking of
Adam's first sin, to try and get *behind* the act of man's will, and
this can get one into trouble. Rome, or at least certain strands
of the Roman Catholic tradition, has flirted (more than flirted?)
with ascribing something fundamentally sinful or evil into the
heart of the created order—'concupiscence,' or sinful desire. That
is, Rome has talked of there being a 'defect' in man *as created*.

Etienne Gilson comes close to this when he writes:

[Adam's first sin] was the spontaneous movement of a nature
drawn out of nothingness by God, one which preceded even the

---

2   *Ibid.*

3   *City of God* XII.21.

4   *Ibid.*

temptation by the devil, because the promise of being like God would not have led man astray if he had not already begun to take delight in himself. *This was the hidden evil which the external act merely uncovered*: his proud ambition to be his own light; his refusal to remain turned towards the true light, even though it would make a light of him.[5]

If Gilson is saying that the *act* of sin was simply the manifestation of a 'hidden evil' that was *inherent* in man *as created*, then we have a problem. For then man as *created* is sinful or evil. If Gilson is making the more nuanced point that Adam's original act of sin was the flowering *externally* of a 'hidden evil' that had (perhaps) arisen *after the creation of a fully good world*, that is another matter. The implications still must be worked through carefully. But the bottom line is that for Augustine and the Christian tradition, God creates a fully good world with no trace of evil or sin.

There seems to be a difference between (1) how Augustine thought of concupiscence, and (2) how aspects of later Roman Catholic tradition have thought about concupiscence. Augustine seems to teach that concupiscence arises *after* the Fall.

Man as Free

For Augustine, man was created not only as a good being, but also a free one. He maintains that man is most truly free (and only *truly* free) when he is not caught up and bound by various sinful desires and temptations: 'The will, therefore, is then truly free, when it is not the slave of vices and sins. Such was it given us by God; and this being lost by its own fault, can only be restored by Him who was able at first to give it.'[6] Even after the entrance of sin into the world, Augustine can still call man 'free'—but only in a certain sense.[7] Man will also be free in his future state, when

---

5   Etienne Gilson, *The Christian Philosophy of Saint Augustine* (Random House, 1960), 151. Emphasis mine.

6   *City of God* XIV.11.

7   We will deal more with how man is still 'free' after the entrance of sin into the world below. In short: man is still 'free' in that man does what he wants. But it is

all sin and evil have been fully dealt with. We will return to that important and *future* sense of freedom.

Man, Happiness, and the Supreme Good

It is common for Augustine to speak of man's goal as to be happy. What Augustine means by 'happy,' of course, is not what we usually mean by the term today. For Augustine, to be happy is to relate to God and to love God in a way that is fitting to who God and man are. Thus, Augustine writes: 'For man has no other reason for philosophizing than that he may be happy; but that which makes him happy is itself the supreme good.'[8]

Augustine goes on to write that only the just man—and ultimately this will be a Christian—can truly attain peace: 'He, then, who prefers what is right to what is wrong, and what is well-ordered to what is perverted, sees that the peace of unjust men is not worthy to be called peace in comparison with the peace of the just.'[9]

Man as Image-Bearer

Central to Christian understandings of man as created is the key affirmation that man was created in the image of God. Augustine writes: 'God, then, made man in His own image. For He created for him a soul endowed with reason and intelligence, so that he might excel all the creatures of earth, air, and sea, which were not so gifted.'[10]

---

a freedom of a certain sort. He does what he wants, but he is certainly shaped and even constrained by his own wants. And certain options—like moving salvifically towards God—require something (i.e., the grace of God) to work from outside of man.

8   *City of God* XIX.6.

9   *Ibid.*, XIX.12.

10   *Ibid.*, XII.23.

Man and Ordered Loves

Augustine consistently speaks of man's loves, whether of the properly ordered or disordered kind. And of course, at the heart of the 'two cities' (see discussion below) are the two loves—either love of self (in the more narcissistic sense) or love of God. Thus, in speaking of the man who has the 'right will,' Augustine writes: 'The right will is, therefore, well-directed love, and the wrong will is ill-directed love.'[11]

True virtue, as Augustine understands it, is 'the order of love,' and 'we do well to love that which, when we love it, makes us live well and virtuously.'[12]

Adam, Grace, and the Garden

Augustine clearly teaches that if Adam had obeyed God in the Garden, he would have brought himself and his posterity into a condition of eternal blessedness. This will be developed in the later Protestant tradition. Augustine writes that God 'had so made [Adam and Eve], that if they discharged the obligations of obedience, an angelic immortality and a blessed eternity might ensue, without the intervention of death; but if they disobeyed, death should be visited on them with just sentence.'[13]

Augustine can speak specifically of 'merit' in relation to Adam's disobedience. God 'created man with such a nature that the members of the race should not have died, had not the two first (of whom the one was created out of nothing, and the other out of him) merited this by their disobedience.'[14] As Augustine is appropriated by both Protestants and Roman Catholics over time, there are different strands of 'merit' theology that emerge. Rome tends to say that we must merit salvation (even if it is God's grace which works in us to merit salvation), whereas

---

11   Ibid., XIV.7.

12   Ibid., XV.22.

13   Ibid., XIII.1.

14   Ibid., XIV.1.

when Protestants speak of salvation in terms of merit, there is a quite dogged attempt to say that *Christ* merits all that we need for salvation, and the sinner *receives* this meritorious work and all of the benefits that follow from Christ's meritorious work. Augustine says: 'In paradise, then, man lived as he desired so long as he desired what God had commanded. He lived in the enjoyment of God, and was good by God's goodness; he lived without any want, and had it in his power so to live eternally.'[15]

In the Beginning ...

At the heart of Augustine's thought—and arguably at the heart of historic Christian theology—is the affirmation that there was once a realm before sin existed. We now live on *this* side of a radical divide—the divide between the pre-fall world and the post-fall world. To understand how Augustine sees the problem of human sin, including its origin, it is helpful to grasp that Augustine's own position developed over time, especially by means of a decades-long literary struggle with Pelagius and the Pelagians.

Pelagius and the Pelagians

Pelagius and Augustinian Grace

Pelagius was a British monk who was a contemporary of Augustine. Pelagius was eager to see the moral reform of the church. It appears that at first he thought Augustine might be an ally of his—in terms of seeking moral reform. Pelagius had travelled to Rome (A.D. 380), and was in Rome when Augustine was there. Although in the same city at the same time, there is no evidence that they ever met.

At some point, Pelagius heard a snippet of Augustine's *Confessions*. The bolded portions highlight sections that he found particularly problematic:

---

15   *Ibid.*, XIV.26.

> My entire hope is exclusively in your very great mercy. **Grant what you command, and command what you will.** You require continence. A certain writer has said (Wisd. 8:21); 'As I knew that no one can be continent except God grant it, and this very thing is part of wisdom, to know whose gift this is.' .... O love, you ever burn and are never extinguished. O charity, my God, set me on fire. **You command continence; grant what you command, and command what you will.**[16]

To his credit, Pelagius understood Augustine—but he did not agree with him. It is God who commands, and it is *God* who must grant the ability to obey what God commands. Pelagius, on the other hand, believed that God commands. But the notion that God must grant the ability to obey what God commands struck Pelagius as outrageous. How could man be free—and God be just!—if God must grant the ability to do what God Himself commands? Upon this question much of the debate between Augustine and the Pelagians hinges.

While there is clear continuity between Pelagius and the Pelagians who followed him, we will start with Pelagius himself, and try to grasp what he said. We will engage the later Pelagian tradition as we look at Augustine's ongoing literary engagement with the Pelagians over several decades.

Pelagius on Romans 5

The key question for the Augustine-Pelagius debate revolves around Adam, and how you or I do or do not relate to Adam and his transgression. Does Adam in any meaningful way affect you or me? Am I considered or reckoned a sinner due to Adam's

---

16 *Confessions* X.29.40. Emphasis mine. The story of Pelagius' visceral reaction to Augustine's 'Grant what you command, and command what you will' is recounted by Augustine himself in *The Gift of Perseverance* (XX.53): 'When these words of mine were cited at Rome by some brother and fellow bishop of mine in Pelagius' presence, he could not tolerate them and, attacking them somewhat emotionally, he almost came to blows with the one who had cited them.'

transgression? Do I come into the world changed or affected by Adam's transgression? These are big questions indeed.

It is helpful that we have Pelagius' commentary on Romans, so we can learn from Pelagius himself. The key passage that concerns us is Romans 5, especially verses 12-14:

> Therefore, just as sin came into the world through one man, and death through sin, and so death spread to all men because all sinned—for sin indeed was in the world before the law was given, but sin is not counted where there is no law. Yet death reigned from Adam to Moses, even over those whose sinning was not like the transgression of Adam, who was a type of the one who was to come.

Pelagius makes four key points in his commentary on Romans:

1. Adam as Example

First, Pelagius contends that when Paul writes 'therefore, just as sin came into the world through one man, and death through sin,' Paul means this in terms of an 'example' or 'pattern.' That is: There is no meaningful connection between (1) Adam and his sin and (2) me and my decision or actions. Adam provides a poor *example* or *pattern*. But there is no meaningful connection or necessary causal link between Adam and you or me.

2. All Men Do Sin—On Their Own[17]

Second, when Paul speaks of death spreading to all men 'because all sinned,' Pelagius writes: 'As long as they sin the same way, they likewise die.' Again, there appears to be no meaningful connection between (1) Adam's transgression and (2) subsequent human transgression throughout the centuries. Each person may, in fact, sin, but he or she does not do so due to any consequence of Adam's actions.

---

17   Or at least most sin, as we shall see.

3. Death Does Not Always Pass On

Third, Pelagius says something quite startling: 'For death did not pass on to Abraham and ...'. So ultimately, death does *not* always pass on to Adam's descendants. As we begin to see how Pelagius thinks, this makes sense. *Of course* death does not 'pass on'– on Pelagius' terms–for there is not a meaningful connection between Adam and you or me. This flows quite naturally from the first two points just mentioned.

4. An Interesting Asymmetry

In Romans 5:15-17, there is an interesting *asymmetry*. What Christ has done for us to the 'good' is many times better for us than Adam's act was 'bad' for us. That is, as bad as Adam's act– and it was very bad!–what Christ has done for us is not simply a *quid pro quo*, a 'this-for-that.' Christ's gracious act and gift does not simply 'balance the scales.' Christ's act for us is superlatively *better* than Adam's act is *bad*. In short: Paul is trying to highlight the radical graciousness of what God has done for us in Christ.

What does Pelagius do? Pelagius takes Paul's asymmetry and flips it around. Thus: Pelagius highlights Paul's asymmetrical point *by downplaying the destructive and universal nature of Adam's trespass.* Thus, instead of–with Paul, it would seem–noting the radical graciousness of what God has done in Christ, Pelagius interprets Paul's asymmetry to *downplay* or *deemphasize* the significance–indeed the universal significance–of Adam's trespass. Pelagius writes: 'Righteousness had more power in bringing to life than sin in putting to death, because Adam killed only himself and his own descendants, but Christ freed both those who at that time were in the body and the following generations.'[18]

---

18   For how Pelagius treats these themes in a pastoral context, the reader is encouraged to read his *Letter to Demetrias*.

The Augustinian Response

If Pelagius hoped that Augustine would be an ally, it is also the case that Augustine held out hope that Pelagius would be a theological friend. But over time it became increasingly clear that there would be no rapprochement between Augustine and Pelagius or the Pelagians.[19]

Augustine responds to Pelagius and his followers in many works. He will be battling the Pelagians until his death (literally), at which point he was still engaged in literary back-and-forth with the feisty Julian of Eclanum.

In trying to grasp Augustine's response to Pelagius and the Pelagians, we will look at four key works:
1. *The Deeds of Pelagius*
2. *On the Merits and Forgiveness of Sins and on Infant Baptism*
3. *Nature and Grace*
4. *Against Two Letters of the Pelagians*

The Deeds of Pelagius

In *The Deeds of Pelagius*, Augustine recounts seven key errors which one Paulinus saw in Caelestius,[20] a Pelagian. Augustine lists these errors, which were debated at a council of Carthage (411 or 412).[21] These serve as a good summary of the heart of Pelagianism:
1. 'Adam was created mortal so that he would die whether he sinned or did not sin.'

---

19   In *Letter* 186 (I.1) Augustine (along with Alypius) is writing to Paulinus concerning Pelagius' work, *Nature*. Here we get a sense of how Augustine's grasp and understanding of Pelagius had changed. He writes: 'For we too not only have loved him but still love him. But our love for him now is different from what our love for him used to be. For we loved him then because we thought he held the correct faith, but we love him now in order that God's mercy might set him free from the views which he is said to hold that are hostile and contrary to the grace of God.'

20   Warfield discusses these seven in 'The Pelagian Controversy,' 299.

21   *The Deeds of Pelagius* 23. See also *On the Grace of Christ and Original Sin* 3 and 4. Augustine was not at this council, and so is relying on testimony. There was more than one 'Council of Carthage,' which is why I speak of 'a' council here.

2. 'The sin of Adam harmed him alone and not the human race.'
3. 'The law leads to the kingdom just as the gospel does.'
4. 'Before the coming of Christ there were human beings without sin.'
5. 'Newly born infants are in the same state in which Adam was before his transgression.'
6. 'The whole human race does not die through the death or transgression of Adam ...'
7. '... nor does the whole human race rise through the resurrection of Christ.'

On the Merits and Forgiveness of Sins and on Infant Baptism

In the years 411–412, Augustine wrote *On the Merits and Forgiveness of Sins and on Infant Baptism*. Augustine addresses three key Pelagian errors in this volume:

(1) Adam would have died even if he had not sinned;

(2) There are some in this life who have absolutely no sin;

(3) There is no transmission of sin to all persons.

Augustine responds to these three points as follows:

1. First, Augustine argues that death enters the world through the sin of Adam, and is not ultimately a 'natural' reality.[22]
2. Second, Augustine argues that after conversion it is *theoretically* possible that one might not sin, but that this claim simply misses the main point of the all-pervasive nature of sin. And, even after conversion, people are not

---

22 As a (now former) Manichee, Augustine would have seen good and evil running through all things (i.e., when he was a Manichee), including the created order. So, creation could have been seen as inherently evil. But as a Christian, Augustine is eager and zealous to contend that all 'things' are good. That is, every 'thing'—in that all things [=all reality] have been created by God—is good. So 'nature'—that which was created by a good God and is therefore good—must be truly good. So, death cannot be 'natural.' We might think of it as 'natural' in our current day existence, in that we see or experience it virtually daily. But Augustine would contend—strongly—that death is not in fact 'natural.' It is an enemy, and is a distortion of the truly 'natural.'

sinless. Why? Because persons do not *want* to be righteous, or without sin. Even Christians do not delight *fully* in the things we ought to delight in. And, since all persons come into this world *already sinful*, there will never be someone who lives their complete life without sin (excepting Jesus Christ).

3. We should note, before explaining Augustine's next response, that on his third point, Pelagius is being rather crafty. Pelagius expresses (feigned?) concern about those who say: 'If the sin of Adam did harm even to those who are not sinners, then the righteousness of Christ also benefits those who are not believers, because he says that human beings are saved through the one man in a similar way and in fact to a greater extent than they perished through the other.'[23] Let's think about what Pelagius is doing here. He appears to be saying something like: '*Surely* it cannot be the case that everyone is affected by Adam's transgression, because that would mean—as "some" are saying—that therefore everyone benefits from the Second Adam's—Christ's—obedience.' That is, even unbelievers must benefit, which would be absurd. Augustine replies to this point by returning to other scriptures where the doctrine of original sin is quite clearly stated:

And thus, if there is something ambiguous about the words of the apostle where he says, *Through one man sin entered the world, and through sin death, and thus it was passed on to all human beings in whom all have sinned* (Rom. 5:12), and if they can be interpreted and given another meaning, are these words also ambiguous: *Unless one has been reborn of water and the Spirit, he cannot enter the kingdom of God* (John 3:5)? Are these words also ambiguous: *You shall call his name, Jesus, for*

23   *On the Merits and Forgiveness of Sins and on Infant Baptism* III.II.2.

he will save his people from their sins (Matt. 1:21)? Is it also ambiguous that *it is not those who are in good health who need a physician, but those who are sick* (Matt. 9:12)? That is, it is not those who have no sin who need Jesus, but those who must be healed from sin.[24]

As Augustine often does when engaging with his opponents, he demonstrates a thorough knowledge of scripture. He 'beats Pelagius at his own game' by showing the limits of Pelagius' reasoning and highlighting the full counsel of scripture.

Nature and Grace

In 414-415 Augustine wrote *Nature and Grace*, in which he responds to Pelagius' *Nature*. In his *Reconsiderations*, Augustine describes the writing of this work:

> There also came into my hands at that time a book of Pelagius in which he defended human nature, with as much argumentation as he could, in opposition to the grace of God by which the sinner is justified and by which we are Christians. I, therefore, called the book by which I answered him, *Nature and Grace*. In it I did not defend grace in opposition to nature, but the grace by which nature is set free and ruled.[25]

Augustine takes Pelagius to be saying: 'Without the cross of Christ a person can become righteous by the natural law and the choice of the will.'[26] Augustine also takes Pelagius to be saying: It is God by His grace who has created all things, including human nature. Thus, man, *by nature*, can obey the Lord and fulfill God's commands. Since man's *nature* is provided by God's grace, Pelagius can say that man—with the 'help' of God's grace—obeys the Lord.

---

24   *Ibid.*, III.4.8.

25   *Reconsiderations* II.68.42 (on *Nature and Grace*).

26   *Nature and Grace* IX.10.

There are two problems here, on a traditional Christian understanding:

1. First, the distinction between *pre-fall man* and *post-fall man* is being ignored (and a big part of Augustine's subsequent response is to highlight that *after* the fall we all start with wounded natures in need of healing).

2. Second, what Pelagius is doing is subtly (or not so subtly?) arguing that man at present needs no *additional* help or grace from God if man is going to obey God, which sounds essentially like saying that man *really* does not need help or grace if he is going to obey God. If we were to put Pelagius' thought in the form of a syllogism, it would look like this:

    a. God has created us, and this is an act of God's grace;

    b. if we follow *nature* (given by the grace of God), we can live a sinless life;

    c. thus, we can live a sinless life by the grace of God.

On the surface, the conclusion of this syllogism looks sound. But the reasoning behind it is poor. Augustine responds to each of these Pelagian points in turn:

a. First, Augustine agrees that creation was an act of God's grace.

b. Second, he maintains that there is a significant difference between pre-fall and post-fall 'nature.' Man cannot, by *nature*, live a sinless life.

c. Third, and even apart from this pre-fall/post-fall distinction, it is inadequate to say that the fact that our created nature comes from God's grace can truly 'count' as God's 'helping' us by grace to live a sinless life.[27] In other words, Pelagius is equivocating in his understanding of God's grace.

---

27   Augustine begins his line of argument in *Nature and Grace*, starting in XLIV.53.

Against Two Letters of the Pelagians

Augustine wrote *Against Two Letters of the Pelagians* in 420–421. This work was one part of a protracted literary battle with the Pelagian Julian of Eclanum. Other related works were *On Marriage and Concupiscence* (begun 418 or 419, completed in 420 or 421), *Against Julian* (421), and *Against Julian, an Unfinished Book* (429 or 430).

There is a lot in this volume, but we will consider only one section relevant to Augustine's doctrine of sin. In this section, Augustine draws attention to 'five praises' of Julian, which are based on three errors:

(1) the praise of the creature
(2) the praise of marriage
(3) the praise of the law
(4) the praise of free choice
(5) the praise of the saints

The errors hidden by these 'praises' are:

1. 'there is no original sin' (seen in the praises of [1] creature and of [2] marriage).
2. 'grace only helps one who has merited it' (seen in the praise of [3] the law and of [4] free choice).
3. 'in the saints this mortal life is without sin and ... it is not necessary for them to pray to God for the forgiveness of their debts' (seen in the praise of [5] the saints).[28]

For his part, Julian accused Augustine of being a Manichee, in that Julian saw Augustine as denying 'free will.' Augustine's response is: 'Who of us would say that free choice was removed from the human race by the sin of the first human being? Freedom did indeed perish through sin, but it was that freedom which existed in paradise and which consisted in having complete righteousness with immortality.'[29] In short, human choice was

---

28   *Against Two Letters of the Pelagians* III.8.24 and following (cf. IV.2.2).
29   *Ibid.*, I.2.5.

not removed from the human race due to the sin of the first man. What was lost was *a certain kind* of freedom: pre-fall freedom.

The key difference is:

- For *Augustine*, there is a deep chasm between pre-fall and post-fall man.
- For *Pelagius*, there is little (no?) significant difference between pre-fall and post-fall man.

Augustine argues in fact that a *truer* freedom—for post-fall man—can only be realized when grace sets a sinner free from sin. And to be set free means having faith, which is itself a gift of grace.[30] Augustine writes:

> The power, then, by which those who believe in Him become children of God is a gift, since the very fact that they believe in Him is a gift. Unless this power is given by God, it cannot arise from free choice, because it will not be free for what is good if the deliverer has not set it free. But people have free choice for what is evil, if either secretly or openly the deceiver has sown in them a delight in evil or if they have persuaded themselves to it.[31]

Augustine summarizes another opponent, Caelestius, as saying: '[T]he sin of Adam harmed Adam alone and not the human race and … newborn infants are in the same state in which Adam was before the sin.'[32] Over against Caelestius, Augustine gives a strident affirmation of original sin, linking the reality of original sin to the need for baptism:

> [W]e read the letters of the pontiff I just mentioned in which he writes that unbaptized little ones cannot have eternal life. Who is going to deny that it follows that those who do not have life

---

30   *Ibid.*, I.2.6.

31   *Ibid.*

32   *Ibid.*, II.4.6

are dead? What, then, is the source of this terrible punishment in infants, if there is no original sin?[33]

Indeed, for Augustine: The reason infant baptism is so important is that there is an original sin which all contract, and this original sin must be dealt with.

Concluding Thoughts on Pelagianism

If Warfield is right, that the Reformation was essentially the victory of Augustine's doctrine of grace over his doctrine of the Church, and since the Pelagian controversy is so central to Augustine's thought and ultimately his doctrine of grace, perhaps it would be good to reflect on a few summative comments on the Pelagian controversy.

1. The more one emphasizes that one only follows *Adam* by *imitation* rather than *propagation*, it is natural that one could easily begin to emphasize that we follow Christ only by imitation, and not by a more profound and intimate and significant connection.

2. Augustine and Pelagius fundamentally disagree on whether there is a true difference between pre-fall man and post-fall man. This almost seems too basic to state, but it is important to note that this fundamental difference runs through much of the Augustine/Pelagius debate. Is creation good? Of course, says Pelagius, and hence man does have the ability to obey God by his nature. Of course creation is good, says Augustine. But one must remember that there is a radical and fundamental fracture that runs through the heart of creation due to the Fall, and this radical and fundamental fracture runs especially through man. Man—and his *nature*—is different after the Fall from what he was before the fall.

3. Pelagius has a lower view of what man was before the Fall. This is tied to the previous point. So, Pelagius sees all man's current failures and sins as not *fundamentally* a rupture in

---

33   *Ibid.*, II.4.8.

man. That is, since there is not a pre-fall realm from which Adam tragically fell—and with Adam, his progeny—there is in a sense a 'lower' view of man *in his very nature*. We might say that with Augustine there is a *grandeur* and a *magnificence* of man that is simply absent in Pelagius. When man—in the present—sins, it is as if Pelagius believes, 'Well, this is simply what man does. Sometimes he obeys, sometimes he disobeys.'

4. Fourth, Pelagius, in his attempt to *secure* man's freedom or liberty, has perhaps constructed his anthropology so as to actually render incomprehensible a meaningful understanding of human freedom and nature. Let me explain. Warfield makes a penetrating observation, suggesting that one of Pelagius' chief errors was his emphasis on:

    (1) *each individual act* of man over against, or at the expense of,

    (2) man's *character*.

Or as Warfield writes: '[Pelagius] looked upon freedom in its *form* only, and not in its *matter*.'[34] Likewise, with Pelagius, 'the will was isolated from its acts, and the acts from each other, and all organic connection or continuity of life was not only overlooked but denied.'[35]

It is worth pausing to grasp the import of this critique. If Warfield is correct, in Pelagius' attempt to safeguard or defend the free individual—by emphasizing the free individual *acts* of the person's will, he is actually engaged in a kind of destruction or downgrading of what it means to be human. That is, in emphasizing the freedom of each individual act of the will, Pelagius did not give attention to how our various acts as persons can shape us over time— whether in a more or less moral direction. As Warfield

---

34 Warfield, 'Pelagian Controversy,' 296.

35 *Ibid.*

could note: 'After each act of the will, man stood exactly where he did before: indeed, this conception scarcely allows for the existence of a "man"—only a willing machine is left, at each click of the action of which the spring regains its original position, and is equally ready as before to reperform its function.'[36] In short, while trying to *secure* the freedom of man, Pelagius may have been helping, conceptually, to *destroy* the freedom of man.[37]

Thus, a certain kind of *philosophical* commitment by Pelagius to the notion of the radical disjunction of a person's individual acts made it virtually conceptually impossible for Pelagius to consider that an actual *person* (and his acts) could be somehow meaningfully tied to the rest of the race.

5. Fifth, Pelagius' way of reading the Old Covenant and New Covenant (only briefly touched on here) reveals a fundamental hermeneutical weakness. It appears that there was virtually no sense of a historical-redemptive reading of Scripture in Pelagius. The great biblical tensions of already/not yet, and of the Law's holiness, righteousness, and goodness, combined with its pedagogical role which culminates in Christ, the end of the Law, are strangely missing in Pelagius. The idea that the Old Covenant was good, but had a fading glory, while the New Covenant is truly *better*, with an unfading glory, seems to have no purchase in Pelagius' theologizing.

Hence, the Bible is essentially a very flat book in Pelagius. This is why Pelagius has no problem saying that surely at least some Old Testament saints would have lived perfectly

---

36 *Ibid.*

37 We will not pursue it here, but it is worth nothing that the French existentialists, such as Camus and Sartre, liked to argue that we are always shaped and determined by each of our decisions throughout life. That is, we find ourselves today as that person who is shaped by all of life's decisions over time. Our actions and decisions throughout life really do matter, and ultimately shape who we are. We are not just—contra Pelagius—willing or acting 'machines.' We are truly persons.

holy and righteous lives. Whereas the Christian church has wrestled with the realities of Old and New Covenant, the ways in which we have moved from shadow to reality, from type to anti-type, similar fundamental biblical categories and hermeneutical queries are strangely lacking in Pelagius' theologizing. Did his hermeneutic lead him astray? Or did fundamental theological commitments keep him from attending to the Bible as he ought? Perhaps things were working in both directions?

6. Sixth, a close study of Pelagius and Augustine forces the Christian—whether an academic theologian or not—to think about the *analogy of Scripture* or the *analogy of faith*. When one studies, for example, the Arian controversy, and the response of Athanasius, we see a strategy of Arius whereby he turns to Proverbs 8:22 to argue that Christ is a creature. Indeed, Arius—rightly!—read the Proverbs Christologically, and thus saw Christ in Proverbs 8. And in *his* text (a Greek version of the Old Testament), Proverbs certainly did seem to portray Christ (i.e., 'Wisdom') as created.

   Athanasius' response was to offer a full-orbed theology of incarnation and redemption, a kind of systematic or biblical theology of sorts, which tried to counter Arius with a theological framework which certainly seemed to derive from careful attention to the Scriptures. Augustine does something similar. Pelagius and the Pelagians do not seem— to me at least—to have been as keen readers of Scripture as Arius was. Nonetheless, in countering the Pelagian challenge, Augustine, like Athanasius, offers a biblical-theological framework over against the Pelagian option, a framework that worked from and cogently illuminated many Scriptures, and was not simply a list of biblical bullet points to counter this or that text used by Pelagius and the Pelagians. Rather, Augustine worked at the deeper level of ultimate convictions, presuppositions, and underlying philosophical premises.

He puts forward a biblical-theological vision that counters Pelagianism in a full-orbed and comprehensive way.

The Reality of Sin

Man the Sinner: So Now Where Are We?

It may seem we have said *enough* about sin at this point. Perhaps we have! We will revisit Augustine's doctrine of sin when we consider his doctrine of grace. For now, let us conclude by reflecting on Augustine's understanding of what it means to be 'free.'

The Fallen Will, and What It Means to be Free

What does Augustine say about 'free will'? For Augustine, fallen man makes no movement toward God apart from God's grace: '[W]e must fiercely and strongly oppose those who think that the power of the human will can by itself, without the help of God, either attain righteousness or make progress in tending toward it.'[38] While we are unregenerate, freedom is ultimately only freedom to sin: 'For free choice is capable only of sinning, if the way of truth remains hidden.'[39]

For Augustine, knowing what we ought to do is not enough. We must also *delight* in doing what we ought to do. As Augustine writes:

> And when what we should do and the goal we should strive for begins to be clear, unless we find delight in it and love it, we do not act, do not begin, do not live good lives. But so that we may love it, the love of God is poured out in our hearts, not by free choice which comes from ourselves, but by the Holy Spirit who has been given to us (Rom. 5:5).[40]

---

38   *The Spirit and the Letter* 4.

39   *Ibid.*, 5.

40   *Ibid.*

When Augustine tries to articulate the plight of the unregenerate person, he often speaks in terms of the sinner's *desires*. In *To Simplicianus* Augustine writes the following:

> The price of deadly pleasure includes the sweetness which deceives, and gives delight in doing contrary to the law, which is all the more pleasant the less it is awful. No one can enjoy that sweetness as the price of his condition without being compelled to serve lust as a chattel-slave. He who knows that an act is prohibited and rightly prohibited, and yet does it, knows that he is the slave of an overmastering desire.[41]

Augustine does believe that man is 'free,' but free in a certain sense. What many call freedom is actually enslavement. Augustine affirms that only through God's grace can mankind become truly free.

---

41 *To Simplicianus* I, First Question, 7.

5

CHRIST, GRACE, AND THE REALITY OF SALVATION

Augustine died close to the time the Christian church was about to finish hammering out its classic Christology: Christ is one person, two natures, and these two natures are neither radically combined, nor radically separated. The Council of Chalcedon (A.D. 451) is generally recognized as the council which settled the question of the two natures—divine and human—of Christ (for comparison, Augustine died in A.D. 430). What does Augustine say about the person and work of Christ?

The Person of Christ

Augustine anticipated what would come to fruition at the Council of Chalcedon: a two-natures Christology that affirms the full deity *and* full humanity of Christ. Augustine self-consciously sought to resist the Arian error, which was to deny the full deity of Christ. At one point in *The City of God*, Augustine criticizes the idea that persons might seek reconciliation with God through demons.[1] In this context, he affirms the full deity and humanity of Christ, and the centrality of His death for sinners:

---

1   This may—rightly!—strike us as an odd notion: seeking reconciliation with God through demons. Augustine is making a Christological point: only Christ can be the Mediator between God and man. But upon reflection, perhaps the notion of 'demons as mediators' is not as counterintuitive as one might think. When

But if (and this is the far more credible and likely view) all men, so long as they are mortal, are necessarily miserable as well, then we must seek an intermediary who is not only man but is also God, so that the blessed mortality of the intermediary may, by His intervention, lead men from their mortal misery to blessed immortality. It was necessary both that this mediator not fail to become mortal and that He not remain mortal. And He did, in fact, become mortal—not by any weakening of the divinity of the Word but rather by assuming the weakness of the flesh. But He did not remain mortal in that flesh, for He raised it from the dead. And the fruit of His mediation is this—that those for the sake of whose deliverance He was made mediator would themselves not remain in perpetual death, even of the flesh.[2]

There is 'but one Mediator, the uncreated Word of God, by whom all things were made, and in partaking of whom we are blessed.'[3] Augustine certainly affirms the sinlessness of Jesus: 'For we were men, but were not righteous; whereas in His incarnation there was a human nature, but it was righteous, and not sinful.'[4] At the same time, he realizes the importance of saying that the Word took on not partial, but full humanity: 'For, to prevent us from seeking one purgation for the part which Porphyry calls intellectual, and another for the part he calls spiritual, and another for the body itself, our most mighty and truthful Purifier and Savior assumed the whole human nature.'[5]

Augustine, like virtually all the church fathers, repeatedly links the person of Christ with the work of Christ, and thus many of his comments on the person of Christ, particularly on the nature of the incarnation, are couched in terms of Christ's

---

persons seek satisfaction and joy in idols, in various sins, might this not be thought of as seeking 'mediation' in things that will never satisfy? Might some persons— albeit somewhat unwittingly—seek their spiritual satisfaction in false gods? That is, in demons?

2   *City of God* IX.15.

3   *Ibid.*

4   *Ibid.,* X.24.

5   *Ibid.,* X.32.

saving work. Thus Augustine writes, 'Christ is the Principle by whose incarnation we are purified.'[6] It is in this context that Augustine affirms the goodness of the flesh: 'Thus the good and true Mediator showed that it is sin which is evil, and not the substance or nature of flesh.'[7] If Jesus was fully human, then it is nonsensical to say that flesh itself is evil.

Augustine is clear that it is the reality of sin which 'necessitates' the incarnation. He writes in Sermon 175:

> There was no reason for Christ the Lord to come, except to save sinners. Eliminate diseases, eliminate wounds, and there's no call for medicine. If a great doctor has come down from heaven, a great invalid must have been lying very sick throughout the whole wide world. This invalid is the whole human race.[8]

This is why the work of Christ is so significant for mankind.

The Work of Christ

What did Christ accomplish for the sake of humanity? One of the key theological terms often used to describe His work is 'atonement': we sometimes say that Jesus Christ 'atoned' for our sins. Augustine speaks of atonement in a number of ways.

Like Anselm of Canterbury some seven hundred years later,[9] Augustine describes Christ as a sacrifice being offered to the

---

6   *Ibid.*, X.24. 'Principle' is used here because Augustine is writing in relation to Porphyry's notion that we are 'cleansed only by a Principle' (Augustine's words).

7   *Ibid.*

8   *Sermon* 175.1.

9   By 'Christus Victor,' I mean that view of the atonement which emphasizes the atoning work of Christ as a victory over death, evil, sin, and Satan. I am suggesting that while Augustine is often categorized as simply an exponent of such a Christus Victor view, there is more to the story. Yes, for Augustine, Christ does indeed defeat Satan on the cross. But for Augustine, Jesus Christ defeats the Evil One not through simple power, but because Jesus Christ defeats the Evil One at 'the justice game.' What is intriguing is that in some of the best (in my view) Protestant theologians' reflections upon the centrality of the penal substitutionary nature of the atonement, the argument is made that yes, the cross does indeed entail a victory over the Devil. But this victory is grounded in, and cannot really exist apart

Father: 'The true sacrifice is owed to the one true God.'[10] He also presents the death of Christ as an instance of expiation, or enabling the erasure of our sin record: 'For He was able to expiate sins by dying, because He both died, and not for sin of His own.'[11] Interestingly, also like Anselm, Augustine can speak of the atoning work of Christ redeeming 'a people so numerous, that He thus fills up and repairs the blank made by the fallen angels, and thus that beloved and heavenly city is not defrauded of the full number of its citizens, but perhaps may even rejoice in a still more overflowing population' (although Augustine does not linger long here).[12]

At a number of points in his anti-Pelagian writings, Augustine is quite clear that salvation is found only in the person and work of Christ. In his comments on Romans 5:12–20, for example, Augustine writes: 'As no one is born in the flesh except through Adam, so no one is born spiritually except through Christ.' Likewise Augustine argues that 'only original sin is contracted through birth in the flesh, but through rebirth in the Spirit we have forgiveness, not only of original sin, but also of voluntary sins.'[13] Augustine is as firm as Paul in seeing the centrality of

---

from, a rigorous commitment to a penal substitutionary and Godward-focused understanding of the atonement. See, for example, Henri Blocher, 'Agnus Victor: The Atonement as Victory and Vicarious Punishment,' in What Does It Mean To Be Saved? Broadening Evangelical Horizons on Salvation, ed. John G. Stackhouse, Jr. (Grand Rapids: Baker, 2002), 67–91. See below, especially Augustine, The Trinity XIII.17.

10   Sermon 374, Sermon of Saint Augustine Preached on Epiphany 16.

11   City of God X.24. I am working from the New City Press English translation here. I am not making any theological point concerning using 'expiation' instead of 'propitiation.' Indeed, in the same section of The City of God Augustine is quite explicit about 'payment' language and 'substitution' language: 'He [Christ] also showed that death itself, although it is the penalty of sin, a penalty that He Himself paid for us without sin, is not something to be avoided by committing sin but rather something to be endured, if the occasion arises, for righteousness's sake.'

12   Ibid., XX.1.

13   The Punishment and Forgiveness of Sins 20.

the two Adams—Adam and Christ—as crucial to understanding a biblical anthropology and soteriology.

For Augustine, as for the larger church, Jesus is both the one who sacrifices and the sacrifice itself:

> Thus He is both the Priest who offers and the Sacrifice offered. And He designed that there should be a daily sign of this in the sacrifice of the Church, which, being His body, learns to offer herself through Him. Of this true Sacrifice the ancient sacrifices of the saints were the various and numerous signs; and it was thus variously figured, just as one thing is dignified by a variety of words, that there may be less weariness when we speak of it much. To this supreme and true sacrifice all false sacrifices have given place.[14]

Augustine argues that it is not the flesh which (by itself) purifies, but the Word which has taken on flesh: 'The flesh, therefore, does not by its own virtue purify, but by virtue of the Word by which it was assumed, when "the Word became flesh and dwelt among us" [John 1:14].'[15]

Augustine speaks of the atonement in terms that today we call 'penal substitution.' For example, Augustine can write:

> For you are displeased with Him who was cursed for us because you are displeased that He died for us. After all, He will then be free from the curse upon that Adam if He is free from His death. But when He took on death from man on behalf of man, He also did not refuse to take on from Him and on behalf of Him even the curse that went with death. For He was of course the Son of God, who was ever living in His righteousness but who died on account of our sins in the flesh that He took on from our punishment. Thus He was ever blessed in His righteousness but cursed on account of our sins in the death He took on from our punishment.[16]

---

14   *City of God* X.20.

15   *Ibid.*, X.24.

16.   *Contra Faustum*, a Manichee XIV.6.

For Augustine, the atonement is not *either* substitutionary *or Christus victor*, but works at a variety of levels. It is interesting to note, given contemporary discussions related to penal substitution, that Augustine does indeed affirm the penal nature of the atonement. Indeed, he at times links penal substitution to the defeat of the devil. Our relation to the devil (in terms of the devil's power over us) is a *penal* [i.e., having to do with a penalty] reality. He writes:

> I mean now to speak of the blessings which God has conferred or still confers upon our nature, vitiated and condemned as it is. For in condemning it He did not withdraw all that He had given it, else it had been annihilated; neither did He, in penally subjecting it to the devil, remove it beyond His own power.[17]

Augustine is at times portrayed as a classic representative of the *Christus victor* approach. He does speak of Christ's atoning work as a victory over the devil. However, it is interesting to note that Augustine sees the victory over the devil fundamentally in terms of *justice*. That is, the devil's influence over persons, and the *reason* the devil has such influence, is fundamentally a *justice* issue. That is: the devil, for Augustine, must be defeated in terms of *justice*.[18] Augustine reasons: 'So it pleased God to deliver man from the devil's authority by beating him at the justice game, not the power game, so that men too might imitate Christ by seeking to beat the devil at the justice game, not the power game.'[19] But how is this so? We noted earlier that while Augustine says clearly that Christ paid our debts, the idea of payment *to* the devil is not prominent. Rather, payment appears to fit under

17   *Ibid.*, XXII.24.

18   For an excellent treatment of the relationship between the 'Christus victor' understanding and the substitutionary/satisfaction understanding of the atonement, see Henri Blocher, '*Agnus Victor*: The Atonement as Victory and Vicarious Punishment,' in *What Does It Mean To Be Saved? Broadening Evangelical Horizons on Salvation*, 67–91.

19   *The Trinity* XIII.17.

the rubric of justice. Augustine asks, 'What then is the justice that overpowered the devil?' His answer: 'The justice of Jesus Christ—what else?'[20]

With this discussion over justice, 'Christus Victor,' the 'power game,' etc., we encounter a good example of why Christians should take the time to go back and read the great theologians. It is simply not accurate to pigeon-hole Augustine as a 'Christus Victor' theologian, then move on. Especially if such a pigeon-holing skims over Augustine's repeated affirmations that atonement is payment and that the atonement deals with God's justice. Does God—in and through the death of Jesus Christ—defeat the devil? Most certainly! But it is not simply an issue of *power*. If it were simply an issue of *power*, why would the death of the Son of God be required? Rather, for Augustine, God—in and through the death of Jesus Christ—defeats the devil in terms of *justice*. And *justice*—not simple *power*—requires the death of Jesus Christ.

Grace in Action: The Nature of Salvation

Perhaps one of the most important questions in the Bible is: 'What must I do to be saved?' This is the Philippian jailer's question in Acts 16:30. It is still a question asked today, and it is one Augustine wrestled with too. Perhaps the best way to get a sense of Augustine's understanding of grace is through his own story.

The Beginning of Salvation

An Intellectual Problem?
Augustine at first claims to have had certain intellectual problems with the Christian faith, such as the apparently unsophisticated nature of the Old Testament and the problem of why evil exists. But he eventually acknowledges that these were not the issue

---

20 *Ibid.*, XIII.18.

at all. Rather, the issue was his will. Augustine writes: 'But in my temporal life everything was in a state of uncertainty, and my heart needed to be purified from the old leaven (1 Cor 5:7f.). I was attracted to the way, the Savior himself, but was still reluctant to go along its narrow paths.'[21] He describes the moment of hesitation:

> But now I was not in vanity of that kind. I had climbed beyond it, and by the witness of all creation I had found you our Creator and your Word who is God beside you and with you is one God, by whom you created all things (John 1:1-3).... And now I had discovered the good pearl. To buy it I had to sell all that I had; and I hesitated (Matt. 13:46).[22]

Augustine's Friends Come to Faith

Augustine recounts in *Confessions* how one of his friends, Victorinus, came to faith. Augustine yearned to have the freedom that Victorinus had, but while at one level he *did* want such freedom, at another level he certainly did *not* want such freedom. Augustine was caught between two competing desires:

> I sighed after such freedom, but was bound not by an iron imposed by anyone else but by the iron of my own choice. The enemy had a grip on my will and so made a chain for me to hold me a prisoner.... The consequence of a distorted will is passion. By servitude to passion, habit is formed, and habit to which there is no resistance becomes necessity. By these links, as it were, connected one to another (hence my term a chain), a harsh bondage held me under restraint. The new will, which was beginning to be within me a will to serve you freely and to enjoy you, God, the only sure source of pleasure, was not yet strong enough to conquer my older will, which had the strength of old habit. So my two wills, one old, the other new, one carnal,

---

21 *Confessions* VIII.1.1.
22 *Ibid.*, VII.1.2.

the other spiritual, were in conflict with one another, and their discord robbed my soul of all concentration.

In this way I understood through my own experience what I had read, how 'the flesh lusts against the spirit and the spirit against the flesh' (Gal. 5:17).[23]

Augustine Approaches Conversion

Though Augustine is torn in two directions and continues to hold back, in Book VIII of *The Confessions*, he tells us that he begins to approach the point of conversion: 'Lord, my helper and my redeemer, I will now tell the story, and confess to your name, of the way in which you delivered me from the chain of sexual desire, by which I was tightly bound, and from the slavery of worldly affairs.'[24] Famously, Augustine asks for chastity, but does not want it immediately! He prays, 'Grant me chastity and continence, but not yet.'[25] He hears of the Christian faith of others (Ponticianus and Antony), and wishes he could break from his sinful desires.

A Battle of Wills

As he nears his conversion, Augustine continues to reiterate his dilemma: the problem is no longer the truthfulness of Christianity. There is a lot one can learn from Augustine. At first—ostensibly—Augustine's problems with the Christian faith were 'intellectual,' but, as mentioned above, Augustine eventually identifies these as problems with his own will, desires, and affections.

Augustine was clearly locked in a battle of wills. He recounts his struggle in great detail, as his 'old self' (or, what will eventually be his 'old self'!) battles with his 'new self' (which was yet to be). This is where Augustine speaks of 'dissociation'—

---

23   *Ibid.*, VIII.5.10–11.
24   *Ibid.*, VIII.6.13.
25   *Ibid.*, VIII.7.16–17.

being dissociated or divided against oneself. Augustine here is extremely helpful for contemporary persons who know intuitively that something is not right but are unable to pinpoint their own problems or the source of their pain. Augustine describes this situation as follows:

> In my own case, as I deliberated about serving my Lord God (Jer. 30:9) which I had long been disposed to do, the self which willed to serve was identical with the self which was unwilling. It was I. I was neither wholly willing nor wholly unwilling. So I was in conflict with myself and was dissociated from myself. The dissociation came about against my will. Yet this was not a manifestation of the nature of an alien mind but the punishment suffered in my own mind. And so it was 'not I' that brought this about 'but sin which dwelt in me' (Rom. 7:17, 20), sin resulting from the punishment of a more freely chosen sin, because I was a son of Adam.[26]

Take Read, Take Read

Finally, after recounting his struggle over a number of pages, Augustine describes his conversion in the garden in Milan. In perhaps the most famous conversion scene in Christian history, Augustine writes:

> From a hidden depth a profound self-examination had dredged up a heap of all my misery and set it 'in the sight of my heart' (Ps. 18:15). That precipitated a vast storm bearing a massive downpour of tears.... I threw myself down somehow under a certain fig tree, and let my tears flow freely.... As I was saying this and weeping in the bitter agony of my heart, suddenly I heard a voice from the nearby house chanting as if it might be a boy or a girl (I do not know which), saying and repeating over and over again 'Pick up and read, pick up and read.' At once my countenance changed, and I began to think intently whether there might be some sort of children's game .... I checked the

---

26   *Ibid.*, VIII.10.22

flood of tears and stood up. I interpreted it solely as a divine command to me to open the book and read the first chapter .... I seized [the Bible], opened it and in silence read the first passage on which my eyes lit: 'Not in riots and drunken parties, not in eroticism and indecencies, not in strife and rivalry, but put on the Lord Jesus Christ and make no provision for the flesh in its lust' (Rom. 13:13-14). I neither wished nor needed to read further. At once, with the last words of this sentence, it was as if a light of relief from all anxiety flooded into my heart. All the shadows of doubt were dispelled.[27]

Grace, Grace, Grace: The Priority and Efficacy of Grace

Having charted Augustine's coming to faith, with its dramatic moment in the garden of Milan, let us look at Augustine's reflections on the *priority* of grace and the *efficacy* of grace. What was the role of grace in Augustine's conversion?

Before the Foundation of the World

It is clear that Augustine did not arrive at his mature understanding of election in a haphazard manner, but had weighed and pondered the issue at some length. In his *Reconsiderations* of *To Simplicianus* Augustine writes: 'I have tried hard to maintain the free choice of the human will, but the grace of God prevailed.'[28]

Augustine can write clearly of divine election at numerous points. For example, in *The City of God* he writes:

> Now, therefore, with regard to those to whom God did not purpose to give eternal life with His holy angels in His own celestial city, to the society of which that true piety which does

---

27 *Ibid.*, VIII.12.28-29.

28 *Reconsiderations to Answer to the Two Letters of the Pelagians* II.1. Notice that Augustine here speaks of 'free choice,' not 'free will.' Augustine could deny that—after the Fall and before conversion—we have 'free choice' (at least in the fullest sense), for our choices are so radically affected by sin. But Augustine could affirm that even after the Fall and before conversion we have 'free will'—we do what we want to do. The entry *liberum arbitrium* in Richard Muller, *Dictionary of Latin and Greek Theological Terms*, is worth reading on these points.

not render the service of religion, which the Greeks call *latreia*, to any save the true God conducts, if He had also withheld from them the terrestrial glory of that most excellent empire, a reward would not have been rendered to their good arts—that is, their virtues—by which they sought to attain so great glory.[29]

In *To Simplicianus* Augustine takes up Romans 9:10-29, wrestling with the situations of Jacob and Esau, respectively. Why did Jacob believe while Esau did not? Augustine circles around the question for some time. Finally, he turns to Philippians 2:12-13: 'Therefore, my beloved, as you have always obeyed, so now, not only as in my presence but much more in my absence, work out your own salvation with fear and trembling, for it is God who works in you, both to will and to work for his good pleasure.' Augustine concludes: 'There he clearly shows that the good will itself is wrought in us by the working of God.'[30]

For Augustine, our 'willing' must flow from God's mercy: 'If God has mercy, we also will, for the power to will is given with the mercy itself.... But because the good will does not precede calling, but calling precedes the good will, the fact that we have a good will is rightly attributed to God who calls us, and the fact that we are called cannot be attributed to ourselves.'[31] Getting to the heart of things, Augustine writes: 'For the effectiveness of God's mercy cannot be in the power of man to frustrate, if he will have none of it. If God wills to have mercy on men, he can call them in a way that is suited to them, so that they will be moved to understand and to follow.'[32] Indeed, 'He calls the man on whom he has mercy in the way he knows will suit him, so that he will not refuse the call.'[33] Augustine writes elsewhere about Romans 9:16:

---

29   *City of God* V.15.

30   *To Simplicianus* II.12.

31   *Ibid.*, II.12.

32   *Ibid.*, II.13.

33   *Ibid.*, II.13.

[I]t remains for us to recognize that the words, *So it comes not from the one who wills or runs, but from God who shows mercy* [Rom. 9:16] are said truly, that all may be given to God, who makes the good will of man ready for His help and helps the will He has made ready. For the good will of man precedes many of God's gifts but not all of them, and it is itself one of the gifts that it does not precede.[34]

Augustine knows that many may question the justice of God when they read Paul's words in Romans 9:16, 18: 'So then it depends not on human will or exertion, but on God, who has mercy.... So then he has mercy on whomever he wills, and he hardens whomever he wills.' Augustine argues that there is no injustice in allowing rebellious humanity to remain in their sin, and there is no injustice if God chooses to have mercy on some:

Sinful humanity must pay a debt of punishment to the supreme divine justice. Whether that debt is exacted or remitted there is no unrighteousness. It would be a mark of pride if the debtors claimed to decide to whom the debt should be remitted and from whom it should be exacted; just as those who were hired to work in the vineyard were unjustly indignant when as much was given to the others as was duly paid to themselves (Matt. 20:11 ff.).[35]

As Augustine continues, note that Augustine—at least here—frames the issue of God not showing mercy to some more in terms of simply passing over them than in 'driving' such persons to sin:

So the apostle represses the impudent questioner. 'O man, who art thou that repliest against God?' A man so speaks back to

---

34 *A Handbook on Faith, Hope, and Love* 32. I find the wording of the last line here a bit cumbersome. I take Augustine to be saying: The 'good will of man' is itself one of God's gifts, and does not somehow 'precede' God's gifts. That is, the good will of man is not a 'non-gift' reality which precedes God's gifts, for the good will of man is itself a gift of God.

35 *To Simplicianus* II.16.

God when he is displeased that God finds fault with sinners, as if God compelled any man to sin when He simply does not bestow His justifying mercy on some sinners, and for that reason is said to harden some sinners; not because He drives them to sin but because He does not have mercy upon them.[36]

Similarly, God 'aids whom He will and he leaves whom He will.'[37]

It is of course in the passage Augustine has been discussing (Rom. 9:10ff.) that we have the potentially troubling text: 'Jacob I loved, Esau I hated' (Rom. 9:13). Augustine begins to speak to this challenging passage by making recourse to God as the creator: 'Every creature of God is good. Every man is a creature as man but not as sinner.'[38] God loves all His creatures, including the unregenerate sinner: 'But God loved in him [Esau], not the sin which He had blotted out, but the grace which He had freely given Him.' God 'hates nothing which He has made,' but rather 'hates their impiety which He did not make.'[39]

Augustine returns again and again to the idea that we seek God because He first sought us: 'But you sought us that we should seek you, your Word by whom you made all things including myself, your only Son by whom you have called to adoption the people who believe (Gal. 4:5), myself among them.'[40]

Augustine is clear that while *certain* of man's righteous acts precede *certain* gifts of God, ultimately the will must be freed by God's grace. And this freeing of the will—through which we receive other things from God—must be brought about by God. Augustine writes:

But since that fall the mercy of God has been greater, since the will itself has also to be released from slavery, ruled over as it is

36 *Ibid.*, II.16.
37 *Ibid.*, II.17.
38 *Ibid.*, II.18.
39 *Ibid.*
40 *Confessions* XI.4.

by sin and death. Its liberation comes not at all from itself but only through the grace of God which is in the faith of Christ: thus, as it is written, *the will itself is prepared by the Lord* (Prov. 8:35 LXX), and by the will man gains the other gifts of God through which he comes to an eternal reward.[41]

It is God Himself who must free the will. Augustine writes in *On Admonition and Grace*:

> For we must understand the grace of God through Jesus Christ our Lord. It alone sets human beings free from evil, and without it they do nothing good whether in thinking, in willing and loving, or in acting. Grace not merely teaches them so that they know what they should do, but also grants that they do with love what they know.[42]

Similarly, Augustine can write:

> The will itself, then, cannot be an upright and virtuous source of life for mortal men unless it is freed by God's grace from the slavery whereby it has become a slave of sin, and is helped to overcome its vices. And this divine gift whereby it [i.e., the will] is freed would be given because of its merits and would not be grace, which is certainly freely given, unless it [i.e., the divine gift] preceded it [i.e, the freed will].[43]

Whenever Augustine speaks of merit he often notes that we never merit any of God's grace toward us. For example, he says: 'But this grace of Christ, without which neither infants nor grown persons can be saved, is not bestowed as a reward for merits, but is given freely (*gratis*), which is why it is called grace (*gratia*).'[44]

---

41   *A Handbook on Faith, Hope, and Love* 106.

42   *On Admonition and Grace* 2, 3.

43   *Revisions* I.9.4.

44.   *Nature and Grace* IV.4.

The Priority of Grace

Augustine worked out his understanding of grace at least in part in the midst of his literary debates with Pelagius and the Pelagians. Pelagius had denied that all persons come into the world with Adamic guilt and corruption and affirmed that we are able to follow the Lord—including turning to the Lord for salvation—without any special work of God's grace. In short, every person comes into the world without any stain of Adam's sin. The Scriptures tell us how to live, and any persons who so chooses can simply decide to start following the Lord. The need for a redeemer to come and rescue me from my bondage and slavery and death is not acknowledged in Pelagius' understanding.

In Augustine's debates with the Pelagians, however, he argued consistently for the *priority* of grace. Why? Augustine did not seek to deny the reality of human willing or acting—contra certain Pelagian criticisms. Augustine's response was that human persons *do* trust in the Lord or obey the Lord. *But*—and this is key—the human act of faith or the human act of obedience to the Lord is never *autonomous* or solely self-generated. These acts never precede God's actions of grace. There is a *priority* of grace, which *then* leads to or prompts human faith or obedience. For example, Augustine can write:

> This then is the purpose of God, of which it is said, 'He works together all things for good for those who are called according to purpose.' Subsequent grace indeed assists a human good purpose, but the good purpose would not itself exist if grace did not work first.[45]

In arguing against Julian of Eclanum Augustine challenges Julian's notion that God simply 'helps' us with grace. He writes:

> For why have you failed to say that a person is roused by God's grace to good work, as you have indeed said that he is aroused to evil by the suggestions of the devil? Why have you merely

---

45   *Against Two Letters of the Pelagians* II.22.

said that a person is always 'helped' in a good work by God's grace? As if by his own will, and without any grace of God, he understood a good work and then was divinely helped in the work itself, on account of the virtues of his good will. In that case, grace is rendered as something due, rather than given as a gift–and so grace is no longer grace. [46]

Augustine continues:

But who is 'drawn,' if he was already willing? And yet no-one comes unless he is willing. Therefore in wondrous ways a person is drawn into a state of willingness, by Him who knows how to work within the very hearts of human beings. Not that unwilling people are made to believe, which cannot be. Rather, unwilling people are made willing.[47]

When we make a good 'resolution,' it is because God has been at work:

They need to understand and confess that even that good resolution itself, which grace then comes and assists, could not have existed in a person if grace had not gone before it. How can there be a good resolution in someone without the mercy of God going first, since it is the good will which is itself prepared by the Lord?[48]

Augustine summarizes his position as follows: 'So then, in everything where anyone does anything in accordance with God, God's mercy works first.'[49] Augustine frequently returns to Ezekiel 36:26-27 as a supporting text:

And I will give you a new heart, and a new spirit I will put within you. And I will remove the heart of stone from your flesh and give you a heart of flesh. And I will put my Spirit within you, and cause you to walk in my statutes and be careful to obey my rules.

---

46   *Ibid.*, I.37.

47   *Ibid.*

48   *Ibid.*, IV.13-14.

49   *Ibid.*

The Efficacy of Grace

We have just seen that in Augustine grace has a certain *priority*. For Augustine, God's grace also has a certain *efficacy*. Augustine repeatedly emphasizes that it is God who enables us to do what we ought. For example, he writes: 'The true meaning of grace, however, is the love that God breathes into us, which enables us with a holy delight to carry out the duty that we know.'[50] Augustine through the course of his writings gives great emphasis to the grace of God in initiating our salvation, helping Christians to grow in grace, and in enabling His people to persevere. In speaking of those who have come to Christ, Augustine also consistently affirms the centrality of desire, delight and affections. That is, consistent with his overarching theology of the will, Augustine contends that persons ultimately do what they want. Whereas before conversion persons do not *want*, ultimately, to believe, in a similar way *after* conversion we obey God because we *want* to. Just as we believed because we *wanted* to, so we walk in grace because we *want* to. Thus, Augustine can write:

> We, on the other hand, say that the human will is helped to achieve righteousness in this way: Besides the fact that human beings are created with free choice of the will and besides the teaching by which they are commanded how they ought to live, they receive the Holy Spirit so that there arises in their minds a delight in and a love for that highest and immutable good that is God.[51]

He continues,

> [U]nless we find delight in it and love it, we do not act, do not begin, do not live good lives. But so that we may love it, the love of God is poured out in our hearts, not by free choice

---

50   *Against Two Letters of the Pelagians* IV.11.

51   *On the Spirit and Letter* 5.

which comes from ourselves, but by the Holy Spirit who has been given to us (Rom. 5:5).[52]

Delight is central, and if one misses this, one misses the heart of Augustine on the Christian life. We *want* to do godly things, for God has transformed our *desires*. Augustine writes in his *Against Two Letters of the Pelagians*: 'For the good begins to be desired when it begins to become sweet.'[53]

And Augustine is clear that the desire comes from the Lord:

> [A] human being would not have the desire for the good from the Lord, if it were not good, but if it is good, we have it from no one but from him who is supremely and immutably good. For what is the desire for good but the love about which the apostle John speaks without any ambiguity when he says, Love is from God (1 John 4:7)? Nor does its beginning come from us and its completion come from God; rather, if love is from God, we have the whole of it from God.[54]

Augustine continues, making the point that the sweetness itself comes from the Lord:

> [T]he blessing of sweetness is the grace of God by which He brings it about in us that we find delight in and we desire, that is, that we love, what He commands us. If God does not go before us with this grace, we not only do not complete, but we do not even begin to do what He commands. After all, if we can do nothing without Him, we obviously can neither begin it nor bring it to completion. For scripture said, His mercy will go before me (Ps. 59:10) so that we might begin it, and it said, His mercy will follow after me (Ps. 23:6) so that we might complete it.[55]

Likewise, God gives us a delight in Himself:

---

52   *Ibid.*, 5.

53   *Against Two Letters of the Pelagians* 21.

54   *Ibid.*

55   *Ibid.*

[T]he good begins to be desired when it begins to be sweet ... therefore the blessing of sweetness is the grace of God, whereby we are made to delight in and to desire, that is, to love, what He commands us.[56]

Christians persevere because they *want* to persevere, even if, for Augustine, *all* they can ultimately do is persevere. Augustine writes:

Now in the case of the saints who are predestined to the kingdom of God by the grace of God, the assistance of perseverance which is given is not that [granted to the first man], but that kind which brings the gift of actual perseverance. It is not just that they cannot persevere without this gift; once they have received this gift, they can do nothing except persevere.[57]

And the will is central. Thus, in speaking of his experience leading up to his conversion, Augustine can write, 'At this point the power to act is identical with the will.'[58]

For Augustine we do not even begin to do good works unless God moves in us. He writes:

But because we cannot do good works unless helped by His gift, as the apostle says, For it is God who produces in you both the will and the action in accord with good will (Phil. 2:13), we shall not be able to rest after all our good works that we do in this life unless we have been made holy and perfect for eternity by His gift. Hence, scripture says of God Himself that, after He had made all things very good, He rested on the seventh day from all the works which He made (Gen. 1:31 and 2:2). For that day signified the future rest that He was going to give us human beings after our good works. After all, just as when we do good works, He by whose gift we do good works is said to work within us, so when we rest, He by whose gift we rest is said to rest.[59]

---

56   *Against Two Pelagian Letters* II.21.

57   *On Admonition and Grace* XII.34.

58   *Confessions* VIII.8.20.

59   *Letter 55* 10.19.

Augustine holds that a person's true identity is determined by the nature of their loves. We ought to love the right thing (not the wrong thing), and we ought to love the right thing in the right way. Augustine writes:

> [F]or he is not justly called a good man who knows what is good, but who loves it. Is it not then obvious that we love in ourselves the very love wherewith we love whatever good we love? For there is also a love wherewith we love that which we ought not to love: and this love is hated by Him who loves that wherewith He loves what ought to be loved.[60]

The Gift of Perseverance

God's grace efficaciously brings about the perseverance of those who are truly God's children. This is worked out at various places in Augustine's writings, but especially toward the last five or so years of his life. One sees this theme in the following works: *Grace and Free Choice* (426), *Rebuke and Grace* (426/427), *The Predestination of the Saints* (428/429), and *The Gift of Perseverance* (428/429). It is also seen in certain of Augustine's letters: especially *Letters* 194, 214, and 215.

Although the Pelagians were never too far in the background, Augustine's doctrine of perseverance was hammered out in part because of interaction with two other groups as well: (1) certain monks at Hadrumetum (in northern Africa, modern-day Sousse in Tunisia), and (2) certain monks in southern Gaul (current-day France), in particular in Marseilles (Provence) and in Lérins (an island off the coast of southern France).[61] We cannot work through every detail here, but we find in this exchange between Augustine and these two groups the seeds of centuries of debate in the Church concerning the issues that arise when one tries to

---

60 *City of God* XI.28.

61 For readers wanting a further introduction to the background of this issue I recommend the introductory essay in volume I, number 26 of the New City Press edition of Augustine's works in English.

wrestle seriously with the sovereign grace of God in salvation. Perhaps one of the most important issues is simply: How can it be that God's salvific grace is truly undeserved, and how can it be that there is nothing in the fallen person which 'triggers' or brings about God's salvific grace? We simply summarize some of the key points in the debate here.

The gift of final perseverance is a gift, and it is indeed a gift given to some, not all.[62] When asked 'why'—why do some receive the gift and some do not?—Augustine wisely says he does not know: '[P]erseverance in the good is a gift of God, and without murmuring against God let them be content not to know along with us why God gives this to some and not to others.'[63] Interestingly, Augustine holds that some persons who have received the gift of rebirth (=regeneration) do *not* in fact receive the gift of final perseverance.[64] Here, as often on these topics, Augustine appeals to Romans 11:33, and speaks of 'the inscrutable judgments of God.'

This is one of those places where the Reformed Protestant will (understandably) scratch his or her head. Regeneration but not necessarily perseverance? This is a place where the Reformed Protestant will need to simply depart from the great Doctor of Grace, as in historic Reformed Protestantism there is a much tighter, closer and coherent understanding of the continuity of the grace that begins, carries on, and completes the salvation of persons.

At other times, however, in Augustine's writings, we *do* see a closer connection between the various movements of God's grace in the sinner. Thus the predestined, the called, those who are made righteous, are *also* those who indeed persevere— and they persevere because of the gift of final perseverance.[65]

---

62   *Rebuke and Grace* 19.

63   *Ibid.*

64   *Ibid.*, 17 and 18.

65   *Ibid.*, 23.

Augustine writes: 'Whoever, then, have been foreknown, predestined, called, made righteous, and glorified in God's most provident decision—I do not mean just those who have not yet been reborn, but also those who have not yet been born—are already children of God and can never perish.'[66] Thus Augustine can write: 'Because, therefore, they did not have perseverance, just as they were not truly disciples of Christ, so they were also not truly children of God, even when they seemed to be and were called such.'[67]

A word should be said about our *ultimate* end in salvation: what is often spoken of as 'glorification.' Since that topic fits so naturally in a discussion of *The City of God*, we will treat it in Chapter Eight, where we deal with Augustine's *magnum opus*.

Augustine and Justification

For traditional Protestant theology, the doctrine of justification is essential. For Luther, it is the article by which the Church stands or falls. For Calvin, it is the hinge of religion. Augustine is a hero for many Protestants. What was his perspective on justification? This is a large topic which we can only broach here.

Augustine could certainly affirm that we are justified by the grace of God, but there is a distinction between (1) the way Augustine spoke of justification and (2) the way the later Protestant tradition would develop the doctrine of justification and speak of this doctrine. For the Reformation tradition, God is the *agent* of justification (God is doing the justifying), Christ's work on the cross is the *grounds* of justification, and the faith of the person is the *means* of justification. When someone believes (when they have faith) God *imputes* or *reckons* that person righteous. God declares a sinner to be right with God (God as the *agent* of justification)—*through* faith (faith as the *means* of justification), *on the basis of* what Christ has done (Christ's work

---

66   *Ibid.*

67   *Ibid.*, 22.

on the cross as the *grounds* of justification). Thus, for Protestants, there is an emphasis on the once-for-all, punctiliar, legal, and declarative nature of justification. Rome will—at the Council of Trent formally and dogmatically—denounce this understanding of justification.

Augustine is writing more than 1,000 years before the Reformation, and so is not concerned to articulate his view vis-a-vis that later conflict. So, it would be unfair to read Augustine as rejecting (or affirming) that later understanding. What we can try to do is simply ask: what exactly was Augustine saying, and how does his understanding relate to the later development of the doctrine—especially as affirmed by the Protestant tradition?

Commentators often point out that Augustine used the Latin word *iustificare*, 'to make righteous,' when speaking of justification.[68] In the New Testament we find various biblical writers—especially Paul—using the Greek word *dikaoō* ('justify,' taken to mean 'to declare righteous' or 'to reckon righteous'). Since the Latin word *iustificare* can be used by Augustine to mean 'to *make* righteous,' rather than 'to *declare* righteous,' many commentators conclude that Augustine's understanding of justification is fundamentally different from the Protestant tradition, as well as from the New Testament—especially from Paul.

Thus the problem—as seen by many—is that Augustine could speak of justification in *transformational* terms rather than in more *legal* or *declarative* terms. What is one to make of this? There is always the temptation to bring Augustine into one's own theological camp, and I will try to resist this temptation.

Once-For-All, Punctiliar, Declarative Justification?

At times Augustine does speak of justification in a more once-for-all, or punctiliar, or even declarative sense. For example, in *On the Spirit and the Letter* Augustine writes: '[Paul] said: "The

---

68   *Justificare* is an infinitive: 'to make righteous.'

righteousness of God has been revealed." He did not say: "The righteousness of human beings or of our own will." He said: "The righteousness of God," not that by which God is righteous, but that with which he clothes a human being when he justifies a sinner' (referencing here Rom. 10:3).[69]

In the same work Augustine says: 'By grace they are, of course, justified gratuitously, that is, without any preceding merits from their own works. "Otherwise, grace is no longer grace" (Rom. 11:6).' Augustine continues along this line: 'It [i.e., justification] is given, not because we have done good works, but so that we might be able to do them, that is, not because we have fulfilled the law, but in order that we might be able to fulfill the law.'[70]

In 12.19 of *On the Spirit and the Letter* Augustine can write of the 'righteousness of God': '[I]t is called "the righteousness of God," because by His bestowal of it He makes us righteous, just as we read that "salvation is the Lord's," because He makes us safe'.[71] In 13.22 of *On the Spirit and the Letter* Augustine writes: 'Human beings are not justified by the commandments that teach us to live well, but only through faith in Jesus Christ, that is, not by the law of works, but by the law of faith, not by the letter, but by the Spirit, not by the merits of actions, but gratuitously by grace.'[72]

In *On the Spirit and the Letter* Augustine touches upon Romans 2:13: '... the doers of the Law shall be justified.' He writes:

He meant nothing else to be understood by his term *gratuitously*, but that works do not precede justification. Elsewhere he says plainly, *If it is by grace, it is not on the basis of works; otherwise, grace is no longer grace* (Rom. 11:6). We must rather understand, *Those who observe the law will be justified* (Rom. 2:13) so that we

69   *On the Spirit and the Letter* IX.15.

70   *Ibid.*, X.16.

71   *Ibid.*, XII.19.

72   *Ibid.*, XIII.22.

realize that they fulfilled the law only because they are justified. Thus justification does not follow upon the observance of the law; rather, justification precedes the observance of the law. What else, after all, does *justified* (Rom. 3:24) mean but: made righteous by the one, of course, *who justifies sinners* (Rom. 4:5), so that from sinners they become righteous?[73]

Interestingly, Augustine here is quite clear: there is an absolute priority to justification, and only from justification does there follow any observance of God's law.

In *On the Spirit and the Letter* we find another interesting passage. Augustine writes:

For a work that brings life to the one who does it is only done by a person who *has been justified*. But *justification is obtained through faith*; scripture says of it, *Do you say in your heart*, 'Who will go up to heaven?' That is, to bring Christ down. Or 'Who will go down to the depth?' That is, to bring Christ back from the dead. But what does it say? 'The word is near to you, on your lips and in your heart' (Deut. 30:12–14). *This is the word of faith that we preach. For, if you confess with your lips that Jesus is Lord and believe in your heart that God has raised Him from the dead, you will be saved* (Rom 10:6–9). [74]

Note: as far as the 'works' of a Christian are concerned, when a 'work' brings life to someone, it is *only* in the life of someone whose 'justification is obtained through faith.' It would be hard to distinguish this particular articulation from a myriad of similar statements found in John Calvin's *Institutes*, when Calvin speaks of how God can 'justify' a believer's 'works,' for a

---

73   *Ibid.*, XXVI.45.

74   *The Spirit and the Letter*, XXIX.51. The Latin here is worth noting: *non fit nisi a justificato*. We might translate this woodenly to try to grasp something of the grammar: 'It is not done unless/except by/from the [one having been] justified.' *Justificato* is the ablative, singular, perfect, passive participle of the Latin verb justifico, justificare, justificavi, justificatus: 'to justify,' 'to make just.'

believer's works are seen as flowing from the life of someone *who is first, foremost, and always justified by faith alone apart from works.*[75]

Augustine's exposition on a couple of Psalms are also intriguing. Augustine broaches the topic of whether our justification follows upon, or can even be earned by, some kind of work. For Augustine this simply cannot be the case:

> No human being can act justly unless first justified; but by *believing in him who justifies the impious* (Rom. 4:5) he begins with faith. Thus his good works do not precede his justification as an entitlement but follow it to demonstrate what he has received.[76]

Augustine's comments on Psalm 32 are striking. He writes:

> *Because the Lord's word is straight.* The straight word of the Lord is able to make you what you have no power to make yourselves. *And all His works are done in faith.* This is said to correct any who think they have attained to faith on the merit of their own works; in fact all the works that have any value in God's estimation are performed within faith itself.[77]

In short, in both of these Psalms works demonstrate what has been received in faith (Ps. 110), and that one does not attain to faith by works; rather, works of any value are performed *within faith itself* (Ps. 32).

In his *Epistle* 194 Augustine at several points affirms the utterly gratuitous nature of justification, and that works do not precede justification, but follow justification. Augustine writes:

> But they had no merits in order to become righteous. For they were made righteous when they were justified. But, as

---

75   See Calvin's *Institutes*, starting in 3.11. I have treated Calvin on this issue in my *Covenant and Commandment: Works, Obedience, and Faithfulness in the Christian Life*, New Studies in Biblical Theology (Nottingham: Apollos; Downers Grove: IVP, 2014), pp. 115-20.

76   *Exposition on the Psalms* 110.3.

77   *Exposition 1 of Psalm 32*, verses 4 and 5.

the apostle says, *They were justified gratuitously by his grace* (Rom. 3:24).[78]

Finally:

> What merit, then, does a human being have before grace so that by that merit he may receive grace, since only grace produces in us every good merit of ours and since, when God crowns our merits, He only crowns His own gifts? For, just as we have obtained mercy from the very beginning of faith, not because we were believers but in order that we might be believers, so in the end, when there will be eternal life, He will crown us, as scripture says, *in compassion and mercy* (Ps. 103:4). It is not in vain, therefore, that we sing to God, *And His mercy will come before me* (Ps. 59:10), and, *His mercy will follow after me* (Ps. 23:6). For this reason even eternal life itself, which we shall certainly have in the end without end, is given as recompense for preceding merits, but because the same merits to which it is given as recompense were not produced by us through our own abilities but were produced in us through grace, it too is called grace for no other reason than that it is given gratuitously, not because it is not given to our merits but because even the very merits to which it is given were given to us. But in the place where we find that eternal life is also called grace, we have in the same magnificent defender of grace, the apostle Paul, the words, *The wages of sin is death, but the grace of God is eternal life in Christ Jesus our Lord* (Rom. 6:23).[79]

When Augustine deals with the Psalms we also see this more punctiliar, once-for-all, declarative sense of justification. Thus, in commenting on Psalm 31, Augustine writes:

> That [Abraham's work which flows from faith] is a great work, but it proceeded from faith. I have nothing but praise for the superstructure of action, but I see the foundation of faith; I

---

78   *Epistle* 194.3.6.

79   *Ibid.*, 194.5.19. This is simply one of the finest of Augustine's comments on grace I have ever read.

admire the good work as a fruit, but I recognize that it springs from the root of faith.[80]

In commenting on Psalm 150 Augustine writes: 'Then we are justified by God's merciful calling and by fear of his judgment' (150.3). Augustine then writes: 'once justified we are healed through God's mercy, so that we may not be afraid of His judgment.'[81]

Now this is interesting, and we note a few salient points:

1. Augustine can speak of justification in the perfective and passive sense: 'We are justified.'

2. Also, Augustine states: 'Once justified, we are healed ...' If justification *includes* or *is constituted* by this 'healing,' then the traditional Protestant would tend to demur at this point. However, if Augustine is more saying, 'once justified' we then are also healed and there is begun an inner transformation and change [=healing], the traditional Protestant can certainly say: 'Sounds fine to me—once one is justified there is certainly a work of God's Spirit which brings about healing, transformation, growth in holiness, etc. I would simply rather distinguish *justification per se* from this other/additional work which God undoubtedly, graciously, and certainly brings about.'

In Augustine's *Rebuke and Grace* we again see the once-for-all, punctiliar, or declarative sense of justification. Augustine can write: 'Everyone then begins to be a son of peace who obeys and believes this gospel, and who, being justified by faith has begun to have peace towards God.'[82] Again, we have the perfect passive participle of 'justify'—in the singular, 'by faith *having been justified*,' or simply shortened to 'by faith justified.'

---

80   *Exposition of the Psalms* 31.3.

81   *Ibid.*, 150.3.

82   *Rebuke and Grace* XV.46.

In 1.14.18 of *The Merits and Remission of Sins and Infant Baptism*, Augustine speaks quite candidly and straightforwardly of the fact that Christ alone is the only one who is fully and ultimately 'righteous,' and that He is the one who must justify sinners. Virtually all of 14.18 is worth quoting:

> For his words concerning Christ, *the justification of one* (Rom. 5:18), express this better than if he said, 'the righteousness of one man.' He is speaking, of course, of that justification by which Christ makes the sinner righteous. He does not set this justification before us as an example to be imitated; rather, it is something that He alone can do. The apostle could, of course, say with correctness, *Be imitators of me, as I am of Christ* (1 Cor. 11:1), but he would never say, 'Be justified by me, as I am justified by Christ.' There can be, there are, and there have been many righteous human beings for us to imitate, but Christ alone is righteous and justifies others. For this reason scripture says, *For those who believe in Him who justifies sinners, faith is credited to them as righteousness* (Rom. 4:5). If anyone, then, would dare to say, 'I justify you,' it would follow that this person should also say, 'Believe in me.' But no holy person could say that except *the Holy of Holies*. He says, *Believe in God, and believe in me* (John 14:1), so that, *because He makes the sinner righteous, the faith of one who believes in Him may be counted as righteousness*.[83]

A few highlights of this significant passage include the following:
1. Augustine speaks of 'that justification by which Christ makes the sinner righteous.' It is unnecessary and unwise to read too much into 'make' righteous (as if this requires an internal/infused righteousness or the like). This is more freight than the Latin verb *facio* (the Latin verb meaning 'to make') can bear.

---

83   It is worth noting that in his *Reconsiderations* (2.33) to this work Augustine speaks of 'the grace of God by which we are justified, that is, become righteous, even though in this life none so observe the commandments enjoining righteousness that they have no need to say in prayer for their own sins, *Forgive us our debts* (Matt. 6:12).'

2. Augustine contends that with justification; this is 'something that [Jesus] alone can do.' Indeed, 'Christ alone is righteous and justifies others.'

3. It is striking how Augustine asserts that if a person [Christ] dares to say, 'I justify you' that it follows that this person should *also* say, 'Believe in me.'

4. It is likewise significant that Augustine clearly affirms that it is faith which is counted as righteousness. This is especially the case when Augustine comments on John 14:1 (which reads: 'believe in God, and believe in me'): 'because he makes the sinner righteous, the faith of one who believes in him may be counted as righteousness.'

Progressive and Developing Justification?

There are times when Augustine appears to speak of justification in a way that might make a Protestant wince. For example, in an important passage in Augustine's *Unfinished Work Against Julian*, Augustine says (and here he is explicitly responding to something the Pelagian Julian had written):

> This justification is not conferred through the forgiveness of sins alone, except according to your newfangled theory. God, of course, justifies sinners, not only by forgiving the evil deeds they committed, but also by bestowing love so that they avoid evil and do good through the Holy Spirit.[84]

Here we should take note. Augustine seems to speak of justification as including, or being at least partly constituted by, the bestowing of love in persons 'so that they avoid evil and do good through the Holy Spirit.' The traditional Protestant certainly *does* see a link between (1) justification and (2) the internal change and transformation of the Christian. The traditional Protestant affirms that in *justification* God declares the sinner righteous. By faith apart from works the sinner is

---

84 *Unfinished Work Against Julian* II.165.

declared to be 'just' or 'righteous.' The justified person is the one in whom God places His Spirit, and is one whom God changes and transforms. John Owen can speak of an 'internal principle' that is placed in the person who believes.[85] Similarly, John Calvin can speak of a true union with Christ that occurs through faith alone apart from works. So the traditional Protestant affirms internal change, and an internal principle that exists in the person who truly trusts Christ.

However, the traditional Protestant does not tend to think of this internal change as being *centered in*, or *constituted by*, justification. Justification indeed is *related to* or *leads to* or *is inseparable from* internal change and transformation. But traditionally Protestants have preferred (and insisted on) seeing justification itself as declarative, legal, and punctiliar, rather than an internal and transformative reality. Interestingly, in the quotation from *Unfinished Work Against Julian* above, Augustine seems to speak of this internal change or bestowal of power as centered in justification.

In one of Augustine's sermons (*Sermon* 158) Augustine speaks in such a way that he seems to affirm *both* (1) a more punctiliar, once-for-all, declarative sense of justification, *and* (2) a more progressive sense of justification. In *Sermon* 158 Augustine asks directly: 'What about being justified? What does it mean, being justified? Have we got the nerve to say we already have this third thing ["justice" or "being justified"]? And will there be any of us bold enough to say, "I am just"?'[86] Good question indeed.

---

85   John Owen, *Communion with God.*

86   *Sermon* 158.4. A bit earlier (158.3) Augustine could also speak of justification in the passive voice and perfect tense. In the passive 'voice,' something happens to the subject. In the active voice, the subject of the verb acts or does something, and the verb takes some sort of direct or indirect object (or the subject simply is, in which case there is no direct or indirect object). I am using 'perfect tense' in the sense of completed action. So Augustine writes: 'Because we didn't yet exist when we were predestined; because we had turned away when we were called; because we were sinners when *we were justified*, let us give thanks to God, in order not to remain ungrateful.'

One can imagine sitting in the church and saying to oneself: 'I'd better say no.' Augustine continues: 'I assume, after all, that "I am just" amounts to the same thing as "I am not a sinner." If you make so bold as to say that, John confronts you: *If we say that we have no sin, we deceive ourselves, and the truth is not in us* (1 John 1:8).' Augustine proceeds: 'So what then? Have we no justice at all? Or do we have some, but not the whole of it? So this is what we have got to find out.'

Augustine knows how to ask the right question, and I suspect in this kind of passage we are getting at the heart of his thinking on the issue of justification—mainly because he is clearly raising the issue of what would it take for someone to say: 'I am just.' Augustine is clear that we are—as baptized and forgiven persons—different than we were before conversion. But we are not yet all that we will be. He writes: 'So if there's something we have, and something we haven't got, we must let what we have grow, and what we haven't got will be completed. I mean, here we are with people who have been baptized, all their sins have been forgiven, *they have been justified* from their sins. We can't deny it' [emphasis mine]. Augustine continues:

> We have been justified [note the passive voice and perfect tense]; but this justice can grow, as we make progress. And how it can grow I will tell you, and after a fashion compare notes with you, so that you may all, each and every one of you, *already established in the condition of justification* namely by receiving the forgiveness of sins in the washing of regeneration, by receiving the Holy Spirit, by making progress day by day; so that you may all see where you are, put your best foot forward, make progress and grow, until you are finalized, in the sense not of being finished off, but of being perfected.[87]

Such a sermon is fascinating and tantalizing to the reader, Protestant or not. Augustine can:

1. Look at his congregation and say 'they have been justified.'

---

87 *Sermon* 158.

2. Say: 'we have been justified.'
3. Speak of 'the condition of justification,' into which his hearers are 'already established.'

But Augustine can also:

1. Speak of having 'some' justice, but also say we attain or receive more. This is a justice that can grow.
2. Comment that we are already established in the condition of justification not just by 'receiving the forgiveness of sins' but also by 'making progress day by day.' What are we to make of this: are we 'established' in the 'condition of justification' by our day-to-day progress? This seems odd. Perhaps our 'condition of justification' is 'established' by our day-to-day progress in the sense that our day-to-day progress reaffirms or confirms our 'condition of justification'? An interesting statement indeed.

We see something similar in *Sermon* 159. In *Sermon* 159 Augustine—referencing *Sermon* 158—preaches: '[E]ven so *we have been justified* after the measure appropriate to our present journey in exile, while we are living by faith, and until we come to the enjoyment of the final vision.'[88] At least at a *prima facie* level, Augustine is here speaking of justification as a past tense reality that has already been received.

Interestingly, Augustine can speak of one who is 'partly justified.' He writes: 'It is insulting, I mean, to pray for martyrs, to whose prayers we ought rather to commend ourselves. They have tackled sin, after all, to the point of shedding their blood. To people on the other hand, who were *still imperfect and yet partly justified*, the apostle says in his letter to the Hebrews, *For you have not yet fought to the point of shedding your blood, as you struggle against sin* (Heb. 12:4).'[89] In context, Augustine is describing the Christian who has been faithful to the end—an

---

88   *Ibid.*, 159.1.1.
89   *Ibid.*

end culminating in martyrdom. Against such faithful stalwarts some Christians can be considered 'partly justified.' Protestants today can affirm that (1) true Christians can and must persevere to the end, but will wisely *not* affirm (2) that the language of being 'partly' justified is a good way to articulate the fact that Christians today are still on a pilgrimage to the celestial city; we are works in progress. Rather, Protestants should continue to affirm the utterly gratuitous nature of justification, its legal, declarative and once-for-all sense, and should look to other categories (e.g., perhaps, 'progressive sanctification') to speak of the fact that Christians today are already sanctified or holy, but not yet as sanctified or holy as we one day will be.

Conclusion

In sum, these six points characterize Augustine's teaching on justification:

1. It is clear that Augustine affirms justification by faith. Can we call this *sola fide*? All we can say for sure is that for Augustine, we are justified by faith. We have no meritorious works (or works at all) which precede faith. We are clearly justified by faith and not by works in Augustine's thought.

2. There is a perfective and passive and punctiliar, or once-for-all, sense of justification in Augustine that appears at numerous places. His use of *iustificatus*—the perfect, passive participle of the verb *iustificare*—is striking. When Augustine *does* speak of works—which always *follow* justification—these works are always solicited by God's sovereign grace. So *even* when we raise the issue of works, such works are (1) sovereignly elicited by God's sovereign grace, and (2) such works only have value because God is so gracious in His posture to such works—He looks favorably at our works because He 'crowns His gifts,' which He has graciously given us.

3. My own hunch is that even though *iustificare* is and indeed should be translated as 'make righteous,' one should take care when drawing the conclusion that *therefore* Augustine clearly denied something like a Protestant understanding of justification. While Augustine certainly may be far from Geneva or Wittenberg, one should look at Augustine's understanding of justification across his corpus, and not draw too large a conclusion from the fact that in English *iustificare* is translated 'to make righteous.' As is true also with biblical interpretation, etymology and basic definitions may or may not always make good theology.

4. Augustine can speak of us being 'justified,' or 'having been justified,' but also seems to say that we grow in justification or that there is an increase in justification over time. While there does seem to be in the New Testament a present and future sense or aspect of justification, 'growing' in justification does not seem to be the best way to describe the New Testament sense of justification.

5. All that being said, when Augustine says that we are 'partly justified,' this is hard to square with a traditional Protestant understanding. Read charitably, Augustine may simply be seeing a basic New Testament reality: there at times seems to be a present and a future sense or aspect of justification. Calvin clearly teaches this, and it even led some Reformers to speak of two justifications. Nonetheless, to be 'partly justified' is hard to square with a traditional Protestant understanding of justification.

6. We should also note that at times Augustine includes not only (1) the forgiveness of sins as centered in justification, or as constituting justification, but also (2) affirms that God justifies sinners 'by bestowing love so that they avoid evil and do good through the Holy Spirit.'[90]

---

90 *Unfinished Work against Julian* 2.165.

It is striking, illuminating, and frankly invigorating to read Augustine on grace. And I would include in this Augustine on justification. Although the Reformers will certainly fine-tune, develop, clarify, and articulate the doctrine of justification in a clearer way, and ultimately, in a more thoroughly biblical and especially Pauline way—Augustine's understanding of justification is strikingly similar to the Reformation view at a number of points. It is not at all surprising for Protestant scholar David Wright to conclude:

> Nevertheless we should not lose sight of the genuine affinity between Augustine and the sixteenth-century Reformers on justification. It is well possible—and I have experienced this— to pass from reading extensively in Augustine's writings of his anti-Pelagian years (which encompass the whole latter half of his theological life as a churchman) to Calvin, Bucer, Cranmer, Martyr, and Knox without immediately being aware that they functioned with a different understanding of *justificatio*.[91]

---

91 David Wright, 'Justification in Augustine,' in *Justification in Perspective: Historical Developments and Contemporary Challenges* (Grand Rapids: Baker Book House, 2006), 71.

6

AUGUSTINE, THE CHURCH, AND DONATISM

Augustine on the Nature of the Church

We have already noted B. B. Warfield's comment that 'the Reformation, inwardly considered, was just the ultimate triumph of Augustine's doctrine of grace over Augustine's doctrine of the church.'[1]

When one reads Augustine on the priority and efficacy of grace, and then reads many of the Reformers on the same issue, one can feel like one is reading from the same playbook. But understanding Augustine's doctrine of the church, and how it is essentially *developed and embraced* (with Roman Catholicism), but *modified or abandoned* (with Protestantism), takes a little more spade work.

In the same essay, Warfield writes:

The most significant fact about [Augustine] is that he, first among Church teachers, gave adequate expression to that type of religion which has since attached to itself the name of 'evangelical'; the religion, that is to say, of faith, as distinct from the religion of works.[2]

---

1   B. B. Warfield, 'Augustine,' *Calvin and Augustine*, ed. Samuel G. Craig (Philadelphia: The Presbyterian and Reformed Publishing Company, 1956), 322.

2   *Ibid.*, 319-20.

Warfield says a bit later, about Augustine being a true catholic:

> In his own consciousness, the two [the doctrine of grace and the doctrine of the church] were one: in his theology of grace he was in his own apprehension only giving voice to the Catholic faith in its purity.[3]

As Warfield sees it, if Augustine's doctrine of grace were ever to be fully embraced by Rome, it would by necessity lead to the dissolution of the Roman Catholic system. He notes:

> Augustine was both the founder of Roman Catholicism and the author of that doctrine of grace which it has been the constantly pursued effort of Roman Catholicism to neutralize, and which in very fact either must be neutralized by, or will neutralize, Roman Catholicism.[4]

So, what did Augustine say about the church? Augustine speaks of both a 'heavenly church' and a 'pilgrim church.' The 'heavenly church' consists of all the redeemed in heaven, as well as angels, while the 'pilgrim church' consists of the redeemed on earth, those 'wandering on earth.'[5] Augustine, like Anselm, sees the redeemed as replacing the fallen angels in order to 'complete' the city of God.[6]

The Roman Catholic doctrine of the Church in Augustine can be seen when he speaks of the forgiveness of sins: 'Indeed, outside the Church they [actual sins] are not forgiven, for it is the Church that has received the Holy Spirit as her own as a pledge without which no sins are forgiven in such a way that those to whom they are forgiven receive eternal life.'[7]

---

3   Ibid., 320.

4   Ibid., 321–22.

5   A Handbook on Faith, Hope, and Love XVII.61.

6   Ibid.

7   Ibid., XVII.65

In his *Handbook on Faith, Hope, and Love*, Augustine depicts the church as 'the rational part of creation which belongs to the free city of Jerusalem.' He goes on:

> Here the whole Church should be understood to be meant, not only the part that is on pilgrimage on earth, praising the name of the Lord from the rising of the sun to its setting and singing a new song after its old captivity, but also that part which has remained with God in heaven ever since its foundation and has never suffered any fall into evil.[8]

The Christian church is, for Augustine, a pilgrim community traveling to the city of God. But it is at the very same time the presence of Christ in this world.[9] He writes:

> The universal Church, then, which is now found on the pilgrimage of mortality, awaits at the end of the world what has already been revealed in the body of Christ, who is the firstborn from the dead, because His body, of which He is the head, is also none other than the Church.[10]

---

8 *Ibid.*, XV.56.

9 A Catholic friend who reviewed this manuscript suggested that my wording 'presence of Christ in the world' is perhaps a bit vague. This friend suggested that for Augustine, 'The Church is, when we are using the language of the body of Christ, the community of those Christ has united to himself in his person.' I take his point. For Augustine, it seems, the church is organically related to Christ (Christ is the head of His body, the church), and this relationship is so intimate and 'real,' that the church can be said to be the (real? actual?) presence of Christ in the world. From my perspective: *On the one hand*, when this presence of Christ in the world is pushed or teased out to mean that what the Church does, *Christ* does—especially when the church is viewed in its institutional and hierarchical sense, one can see how Rome sees the doctrinal and ethical teachings of the Pope (when he speaks ex cathedra—from his official teaching 'chair') as authoritative, even infallible. *On the other hand*, when this presence of Christ is seen to be expressed in the worldwide body of those who have been united to Christ by faith apart from works, and Christ through His Spirit is at work in various real but fallible agents who are attempting to love God and neighbor both through word and deed, one is likely moving toward a more Protestant understanding of the Church.

10 *Letter 55*, 2.3.

Warfield suggests that there are two streams or trajectories within the earlier centuries of the Church (before, during, and following Augustine). These two streams/trajectories are:

1. The Church as the *congregatio sanctorum* (the 'congregation of the saints').
2. The Church more identified with the *episcopate*.[11]

Warfield goes on to suggest that Augustine does not carefully distinguish:

1. The *ideal* Church (or the Church as all those who truly know and love Christ).
2. The *empirical* Church (or the 'hierarchically organized Church').[12]

As Warfield sees it, Augustine could often conflate these two, or be using *one term* where *the other term* might have worked better. Or: be *thinking of one reality* while nonetheless *using the other term*.

So, when we get to the Donatist controversy:

1. The *Donatists* emphasized the *pure* Church (think 'the *ideal* Church' above).
2. Augustine countered the Donatists by emphasizing the *visible* Church (think 'the *empirical* Church' above).

Warfield notes:

> [T]he conception of the Church as the sole sphere of salvation, passing into the conception of the Church as the sole mediatrix of grace, and therefore the sole distributor of salvation, was necessarily thrown into high emphasis; and the logic of the situation too directly and too powerfully identified this Church

---

11 Warfield suggests that this emphasis on the episcopate is more fundamental to Cyprian— 'there is no salvation outside the church'—than to Augustine.

12 Warfield, 'Augustine,' 314.

with the empirical Church for the deeper-lying conception of the *congregatio sanctorum* to remain in sight.[13]

Warfield continues: 'Thus Augustine, almost against his will, became the stay of that doctrine of the Church as the sole instrument at once of true knowledge of the divine revelation and of saving grace, which provides the two *foci* about which the ellipse of Roman Catholic doctrine revolves.'[14] What Warfield appears to be saying is that Augustine—even if he did not *set out* to advance a doctrine of the Church that would develop into the Roman Catholic doctrine of the Church we see today— did so. Warfield writes:

> [T]he main stream of Augustine's influence flowed meanwhile in the traditionalist channel, and gave the world the Church as the authoritative organ of divine truth and the miraculous vehicle of saving grace, through which alone the assured knowledge of the revelation of God could be attained, or the effective operations of His redeeming love experienced.[15]

In other words, Warfield contends that if Augustine's doctrine of grace is worked out consistently, this is *fundamentally* at odds with the Roman Catholic doctrine of the Church. In Augustine's own mind there was (as Warfield sees it), never a problem. But in reality—again as Warfield sees it—there is a fundamental

---

13   *Ibid.*

14   *Ibid.*

15   *Ibid.*, 315. There is much more to be said here. I have been helped in my attempts to understand Roman Catholicism by the Italian theologian Leonardo de Chirico, who wrote the foreword to this volume. De Chirico has argued that many twentieth-century attempts to understand Roman Catholic thought—especially Roman Catholic thought since Vatican II (1962–1965)—have fallen short due to their general failure to see the fundamentally systemic nature of Roman Catholic theology. As de Chirico sees it, there are two axioms at the heart of Roman Catholic theology: (1) a nature-grace continuum, and (2) the notion of the Church as the ongoing presence of Christ in the world. See his *Evangelical Theological Perspectives on Post-Vatican II Roman Catholicism*, volume 19, Religions and Discourse (Oxford: Peter Lang, 2003).

antithetical relationship between (1) Augustine's doctrine of grace and (2) Augustine's doctrine of the Church.

It is interesting to speculate how Western Christianity would have developed after Augustine's time if not only his doctrine of *grace* had prevailed (which at the Protestant Reformation it did, if Warfield's analysis is correct), but also *a* certain strand of his doctrine of the Church. That is, one way of understanding the Protestant movement, particularly in its Baptist forms, is as a working out of the notion of the Church as the gathering of believers.

Warfield contends that this notion of the Church as the gathering of believers is *one way* in which Augustine thought about the Church. The *more* one emphasizes the Church as the gathering of believers, and the *less* one emphasizes the Church as a hierarchical, institutional structure centered in the episcopate—a structure where grace is mediated through the priests and attendant sacraments, and where teaching comes (virtually only) through the hierarchical priesthood—the more one is apt to have sympathies with a generally Protestant vision of Christianity and with the claim that grace can be and is worked out in the world in other ways than the hierarchical and (Roman Catholic) priestly channels of the Church.

Sacraments

In his theology of the Church, Augustine laid the groundwork for later medieval developments (and beyond) of a theology of the sacraments. It is not easy to briefly summarize Augustine's understanding of the sacraments. Nonetheless, one essential point is that, for Augustine, a sacrament is a *visible* sign of an *invisible* reality. It is worth noting that it takes work and development to move from (1) Augustine's notion of the sacrament as a visible sign of an invisible reality to (2) the medieval, then later and even current Roman Catholic system in which sacraments are the vehicles of grace coming to persons through a hierarchical and sacerdotal (priestly) structure.

The eternal destiny of Christians is to one day see God face-to-face (1 Cor 13:12), and Augustine's understanding of sacraments must be seen in light of that face-to-face vision. The sacraments are means by which we are drawn *through* visible and earthly things *to* invisible things (i.e., God). Augustine writes:

> [T]he more [the human soul] draws close to [that immutable wisdom] with the disposition of piety, the more the exterior self is corrupted, while the interior self is renewed more from day to day, and all that light of the mind that was turned toward lower things turns back to higher ones and is in some way removed from the things of earth in order that it may die more and more to this world and that its life may be hidden with Christ in God.[16]

For Augustine all of creation in some sense testifies to its Creator, but only some things should properly be called 'sacraments.' He writes:

> Thus with the freedom of Christians we use the rest of creation, the winds, the sea, the earth, birds, fishes, animals, trees, and human beings in many ways for speaking, but for the celebration of the sacraments we use only a very few, such as water, wheat, wine, and oil.[17]

Augustine can speak in intriguing ways about the nature of a sacrament. In *City of God* he speaks—as he often does—of the sacraments as *visible* signs of *invisible* grace (and note that Augustine appears to use the term *sacrifice* for what elsewhere he labels a *sacrament*):

---

16   *Letter 55*, 5.8. Richard Gaffin is very helpful here. In Gaffin's *By Faith, Not by Sight*, he offers a certain understanding of the 'outer' and 'inner' self which is worth careful study. Cf. Richard B. Gaffin, Jr., *By Faith, Not by Sight: Paul and the Order of Salvation* (Milton Keynes, UK: Paternoster Press, 2006), 53–58.

17   *Ibid.*, 7.13.

Some people suppose that visible sacrifices are appropriate for other gods, but that God—since He is invisible, greater, and better—should be offered invisible, greater, and better sacrifices, sacrifices such as the service of a pure mind and a good will. These people, however, obviously do not understand that these visible sacrifices are signs of invisible sacrifices in the same way that spoken words are signs of things. Therefore, just as in the case of prayer and praise we direct to God words that signify and offer to Him the things in our hearts that are signified by our words, so also we should understand that, in the case of sacrifice, visible sacrifice is to be offered only to God and that, in our hearts, we should present our very selves as an invisible sacrifice to Him.[18]

Augustine can also write of sacraments: 'A sacrifice, therefore, is the visible sacrament or sacred sign of an invisible sacrifice.'[19] Interestingly, Augustine can have a broad understanding of 'sacrifice.' Augustine also notes, 'Thus a true sacrifice is every work which is done that we may be united to God in holy fellowship, and which has a reference to that supreme good and end in which alone we can be truly blessed.'[20]

---

18   *City of God* X.19.

19   *Ibid.*, X.5. Note again: sacrifice and sacrament are used virtually interchangeably.

20   *Ibid.*, X.6. Robert Letham makes an intriguing (if a tad cheeky) comment in reference to Eastern Orthodoxy and its love of icons, which might be somewhat made in relationship to Augustine at this point. Letham suggests that Reformed Protestants might be seen as even more committed to 'icons' (and more biblically and rightly committed) than Eastern Orthodoxy. That is, the Reformed Protestant believes that *all creation* testifies to the reality and glory of God. All creation is, rightly considered, 'iconic'—in the sense that all creation testifies to who God is (or, perhaps better put: God reveals Himself through every aspect of the created order). Cornelius Van Til can even say that such revelation through creation (what is often called 'general revelation'), is actually 'infallible': this 'natural' revelation is *revelation*, and does not just reveal to man that there might be a God. Rather, as Romans 1 teaches, God has spoken to every person (and continues to do so). This revelation is 'infallible' in that God infallibly reveals Himself to every person who comes into the world. Again, this is centered in Romans 1:18-32, where all persons actually *know* God (though not salvifically), yet suppress this knowledge. It is because of this suppression that the wrath of God is being revealed against all ungodliness, and hence the radical need of the gospel. See Robert Letham's

Augustine could use the term 'sacrament' (Latin, *sacramentum*) in various ways, but we will give attention to baptism and the Lord's Supper, as Augustine himself briefly singles these out in *On Christian Doctrine*.[21]

Baptism

Augustine is clear in teaching that baptism removes original sin.[22] Indeed: '[W]ithout that sacrament [i.e., baptism] no one enters the kingdom of God.'[23] And Augustine argues that infants who die without baptism are therefore lost. Augustine uses related illustrations to speak of God's sovereign grace: The child of a believer who dies apart from baptism is lost, while the child of the most wicked unbeliever is by God's grace saved. He writes:

> And yet the providence of God, for whom the hairs of our head are numbered and without whose will not even a sparrow falls to the earth, is not subject to fate, nor is it impeded by chance events or defiled by any injustice. Yet His providence does not take care of all the infants of His own children so that they may be reborn for the heavenly kingdom but does take care of the infants of some unbelievers. This infant, born of believing parents and welcomed with the joy of parents, suffocated by the sleepiness of its mother or nurse, becomes a stranger to and is excluded from the faith of his parents; that infant is born of wicked adultery, exposed by the cruel fear of its mother, taken up by the merciful goodness of strangers, baptized out of their

---

book, *The Holy Trinity: In Scripture, History, Theology, and Worship* (Phillipsburg, New Jersey: Presbyterian and Reformed Publishers, 2004) and Cornelius Van Til's essay 'Nature and Scripture,' found in a number of places, but most recently in Peter Lillback and Richard B. Gaffin, Jr., *Thy Word Is Still Truth: Essential Writings on the Doctrine of Scripture from the Reformation to Today* (Phillipsburg, NJ: Presbyterian and Reformed Publishers), 2013.

21   *On Christian Doctrine* III.9.13.

22   This is an example of where, in my opinion, the Evangelical simply should not follow Augustine.

23   *Rebuke and Grace* 19.

Christian concern, and becomes a member and partaker of the eternal kingdom.[24]

Augustine is clear that baptism is necessary to take away original sin.[25] Augustine argues strenuously that the fact that Christians bring their infants to be baptized shows that these adults do in fact know at some level that even infants are sinful. And since this sinfulness is not due to the sinful actions or behavior of infants, such infants must be in fact subject to original sin. As Augustine writes:

> [I]f they are not held by any bond of sinfulness stemming from their origin, how did Christ, who died for the sinners, die for these infants who obviously have done nothing sinful in their own lives? If they are not afflicted by the disease of original sin, why do those caring for them bring them out of a holy fear to Christ the physician, that is, to receive the sacrament of eternal salvation?[26]

In *The Punishment and Forgiveness of Sins and the Baptism of Little Ones*, Augustine writes:

> Mother Church has no doubt that this takes place in little ones by means of the sacrament; she offers them her maternal heart and lips so that they may be initiated in the sacred mysteries, because they cannot yet believe unto righteousness with their own heart or make profession with their own lips unto salvation. And no believer hesitates to call them believers—a name which is, of course, taken from believing. And yet, it was not these little ones themselves, but others who made the responses for them during the sacred rites.[27]

---

24   *Letter 194 (to Sixtus)* 32.

25   *A Handbook on Faith, Hope, and Love* 64.

26   *The Punishment and Forgiveness of Sins* 23. Notice that for Augustine, when one brings the infant to the sacrament (i.e., baptism), one is bringing the infant to 'Christ the physician.'

27   *The Punishment and Forgiveness of Sins and the Baptism of Little Ones* I.25.37.

A few things are worth noting:

1. When Augustine says '*this* takes place in little ones by means of the sacrament ...' it is clear he is talking about 'belief' in Christ itself.

2. Augustine is saying that those who have experienced the sacraments should be called 'believers' (i.e., 'no believer hesitates to call them believers ...').

3. At the same time: there is a sense in which 'others' (e.g. parents? Close friends? God-parents?) are the ones truly believing 'for' the infants during the sacred rites.

We see here a tension in Augustine, and—in my opinion—a place where the Evangelical should not follow Augustine. Lutherans would be the closest to Augustine, with their own construal of baptismal regeneration. But virtually all other Evangelicals will be less inclined to follow Augustine here. As the Evangelical movement took shape in the years during and after the Reformation, Evangelicals put a high priority on the link between personal faith and the Christian life or experience. This emphasis on the utter necessity of personal, saving faith seems, in the history of the Christian Church, to have led many Christians away from notions of baptismal regeneration.

The Lord's Supper

Perhaps one of the most famous places where Augustine speaks of the Lord's Supper is in *The City of God* X.6. Augustine speaks of the sacrifice of Christ and writes: 'Thus a true sacrifice is every work which is done that we may be united to God in holy fellowship, and which has a reference to that supreme good and end in which alone we can be truly blessed.'[28] Thus, for Augustine, when we act as we ought, and act in such a way as to glorify God, that is a 'sacrifice.'[29] Augustine can speak of the life

---

28   *City of God* X.6.

29   *Ibid*. One might think of Romans 12:1 here.

of an individual Christian as a sacrifice: 'Thus a person who is consecrated in the name of God and is vowed to God, insofar as he dies to the world so that he may live to God, is himself a sacrifice.' And Augustine writes about the 'sacrifices' that we as Christians offer:

> [T]rue sacrifices are works of mercy to ourselves or others, done with a reference to God, and since works of mercy have no other object than the relief of distress or the conferring of happiness, and since there is no happiness apart from that good of which it is said, 'It is good for me to be very near to God,' it follows that the whole redeemed city, that is to say, the congregation or community of the saints, is offered to God as our sacrifice through the great High Priest, who offered Himself to God in His passion for us, that we might be members of this glorious head, according to the form of a servant.[30]

And this is where things get interesting. Augustine in this section speaks of sacrifice, and of how all we do that is directed toward God is a kind of sacrifice. *Then* Augustine writes: 'And this also is the sacrifice which the Church continually celebrates in the sacrament of the altar.' Augustine has just quoted Romans 12:3-6, on how Christians are the body of Christ. Thus, when Augustine writes that '*this* is the sacrifice,' he seems to have in mind the Church existing as the body of Christ. Augustine goes on to write that the 'sacrament of the altar' is likewise a sacrifice, for in this sacrament (i.e., the Lord's Supper), 'she herself [i.e., the Church] is offered in the offering she makes to God.'[31]

We should note a few things briefly. A Roman Catholic interpreter may see the seeds (even the explication of) a Roman Catholic understanding of the 'real presence' of Christ in the Lord's Supper. Roman Catholic Joseph Rickaby writes: 'Are we listening to a Father of the fifth century or to the Council of Trent, Sess. 22? And further—to bring together old and new

30 *Ibid.*
31 *Ibid.*

in what is every one and the same Church—we find here the essential groundwork of the devotion known to Catholics as the Morning Offering of the Apostleship of Prayer.'[32] A Protestant might look at this passage and conclude: (1) the life itself of a Christian—if we are truly devoted to God—is a sacrifice; (2) all that we do—if done for God—can be, or is, a 'sacrament'; (3) in the Lord's Supper the Christian Church herself is offered to God.[33]

In short, the terms 'sacrifice' and 'sacrament' are used fairly broadly in Augustine's thought. To the extent that one emphasizes (1) Augustine's broader sense of sacrifice and sacrament, the notion that one's holy life, and all things done for God, are sacrifices or sacraments, one will be less likely inclined to see Augustine as *simply* the architect of what will later emerge into fully developed Roman Catholic sacramentalism. That is: when 'sacrifice' and 'sacrament' are seen in a broader sense as what one offers to the Lord in the course of one's life, then there is less theological pressure to see Augustine as simply one more example of the kind of sacramentalism we see in Roman Catholicism today. However, to the extent that one emphasizes (2) that the Church's self-sacrifice in the sacrament of the altar is also a sacrifice where Christ is really present—and is sacrificed [or actually 're-presented' again]—one will perhaps see Augustine more as a forerunner and early advocate of what will emerge into fully developed Roman Catholic sacramentalism.

---

32   Joseph Rickaby, *Augustine's City of God: A View of the Contents* (Eugene, OR: Wipf and Stock, 2008), 44.

33   The editor of the New City Press edition of *City of God* seems to recognize this privileging—in a sense—of the life and acts of a Christian as 'sacraments.' The editor writes: 'It seems from Augustine's phrasing that "the sacrament of the altar," which is the eucharist or the sacramental body of Christ, is secondary to the sacrifice that is "we ourselves." But it would be correct to say that the sacrifice of the eucharist subsumes or represents the sacrifice of the body of Christ that is the faithful, or "we ourselves."' (footnote 36 from *City of God* X.6).

The Challenge of Donatism[34]

It is appropriate to broach the issue of Donatism while discussing Augustine's understanding of the church and sacraments. Donatism might be understood at a certain level as a movement rooted in the desire for a pure Church.[35] The historical roots of Donatism are to be found in the persecution of Christians that took place under the emperors Diocletian and Maximian between A.D. 303 and 305. During these times of persecutions, some persons ultimately renounced the faith to evade danger, while other Christians endured persecution—at times to the point of death. But what should be done—if anything—with 'traitors' who succumbed to the temptation to renounce the faith, or to hand over copies of Scripture to the authorities to be burned (or even assisted the authorities in other ways), after the persecution had ended?[36]

The Donatist position is that those who 'strayed' during the times of persecution have revealed their true colors: they are not part of the faithful and should not be received back into the Church. It might be a bit challenging for the modern reader immediately to see exactly what the problem is with Donatism. The Christian Church has always contained within her various renewal movements a desire to call the Church back to her 'first love.' Do the Donatists perhaps have a valid point?

The heart of the issue concerns the status of the ministry of those persons who had been *traditores*, 'traitors' (the 'hander-

---

34   Readers might be interested in the work of Leonard Verduin, *The Reformers and Their Stepchildren* (Grand Rapids: Eerdmans, 1964).

35   A standard helpful work on the Donatists is W. H. C. Frend, *The Donatist Church: A Movement of Protest in Roman North Africa* (Oxford: Oxford University Press, 1952).

36   Serge Lancel (*Augustine*, 164-65) writes of one Gallonius of Thimidia Regia, who was told by Annullinus to surrender his copies of the Scriptures: 'When Anullinus asked him to hand over the Scriptures, Gallonius replied that he had hidden them in a place known only to him, and he stuck to his guns even when, on the rack, his flesh was torn with iron claws.' Anullinus would eventually have Gallonius burned at the stake for refusing to hand over the Scriptures.

overs' during the time of persecution). If one had been ordained or baptized by such a 'traitor,' did one's ordination or baptism 'count'? The Donatists did not recognize such ordination nor such baptisms. Thus, the Donatists did not recognize the ordination of someone ordained by a 'traitor,' and would require re-baptism for persons who had been baptized by a traitor. Such questions are, at least, the most pressing and practical questions that emerge in light of a 'purifying' movement like Donatism.[37] W. H. C. Frend summarizes the situation:

> The Donatist writer of the *Acta*[38] records that while in prison the confessors [those persons refusing to hand over the Scriptures] held a meeting among themselves, at which they condemned the *traditor* clergy in the strongest terms. Even to alter a single letter of the Scriptures was a crime, but contemptuously to destroy the whole at the command of pagan magistrates was to merit eternal punishment in Hell. Whoever, therefore, maintained communion with the *traditores*, they said, would not participate with them in the joys of Heaven. In making these claims, the confessors were following in the footsteps of the confessor in the Decian persecution [i.e., A.D. 250], but instead merely of assuming the right of pardoning the lapsed, they were now condemning bishops, among them their own Bishop Fundanus. The whole hierarchical principle was being attacked.[39]

While Augustine did engage in persuasion and activism to try to quell the Donatist movement, and to attempt to win the Donatists back to the traditional Catholic Church, we are more concerned here with the nature of his theological response. Most significantly, while the Donatists would argue for a 'pure'

---

37 For a helpful summary of Donatism, see the article by R. A. Markus, 'Donatus, Donatism,' in Fitzgerald, *Augustine Through the Ages*, 284-87.

38 This is the *Acta Saturnini*. 'Acta' would be translated into English as 'deeds.' This is a Latin document summarizing the 'deeds' (here centered especially on suffering and martyrdom) of certain persons.

39 Frend, *The Donatist Church*, 10.

Church, Augustine would argue for a 'mixed Church' in the here and now, and he utilized the parable of the wheat and tares (Matt. 13:24-30) to illustrate that God will separate believer and unbeliever at some future date. It can be argued that for Augustine, only believers in Christ can truly be considered part of the Church, but his view is that there is little benefit in making hard and fast judgements in the present on who is truly a member of the body of Christ and who is not.

But perhaps most important for grasping Augustine's understanding of the sacraments (and for getting a sense of his influence on the Western tradition that follows him) is his position on the efficacy of the sacraments. For the Donatist, a significant moral failing (i.e., having been a 'traitor' during persecution) rendered that minister's former (and present) priestly work (baptism is particularly in view here) null and void. What is Augustine's response? Augustine will argue that the efficacy of the sacraments does not in fact depend on the moral or spiritual state of the priest, because the *real* or *ultimate* minster ministering the sacrament is Christ Himself, who ministers *through* the 'lower' or earthly minister. Augustine writes that the person 'whom a drunkard baptized, or those whom a murderer baptized, those whom an adulterer baptized, if it were the baptism of Christ, were baptized by Christ.'[40] Augustine continues: 'Jesus, therefore, is still baptizing; and so long as we continue to be baptized, Jesus baptizes. Let a man come without fear to the minister below; for he has a Master above.'[41] Augustine's position is that it is not the purity or holiness of the earthly representative of Christ that matters. Rather, it is the work of Christ, which happens by means of those appointed to serve Him.

---

40   *Tractates on the Gospel of John* 5.18.

41   *Ibid.* Emmanuel J. Cutrone's 'Sacraments' article in Fitzgerald, *Augustine Through the Ages* is helpful in outlining Augustine on the sacraments.

Augustine and the Use of Force with the Donatists

The story of Augustine and the Donatists is a fascinating one—wherever one lands on various issues.[42] The Catholics and Donatists had co-existed together for some time in North Africa, often with Catholic and Donatist congregations in the very same city, as was the case in Carthage. Emperor Constantine and his sons had struggled to bring unity to the African church, with Constantine's sons (in A.D. 346-348) officially supporting the Catholics and even engaging in a military campaign against the Donatists.

In A.D. 405, under pressure from Catholics, new pressure was brought against the Donatists when the emperors brought forth the Edict of Unity.[43] This edict, among other things, outlawed rebaptism—which was, in effect, a virtual outlawing of Donatism. The penalties for such baptisms were: (1) confiscation of property of Donatist congregations; and (2) confiscation of property of those who allowed Donatists to congregate on one's land. The Edict of Unity also included: (1) whipping for persons in the lower classes; (2) removal of the right to bequeath or inherit property in certain situations; (3) freedom for rebaptized slaves; and (4) various sanctions against provincial staff who did not uphold these laws.

Augustine was not a civil servant, but he did eventually approve of the use of such force against the Donatists, for such force could be used by God for their spiritual benefit.[44] Indeed, to *not* use force would have actually been to return evil for evil: 'For, if anyone sees his enemy out of his mind due to dangerous fevers run toward a cliff, would he not repay evil with evil if he allowed him to run in that way rather than if he took care

42 Cf. Maureen Tilley's 'General Introduction,' in *The Donatist Controversy I*, vol. 21, *The Works of Saint Augustine*, translated by Maureen Tilley and Boniface Ramsey, edited by Boniface Ramsey and David G. Hunter (Hyde Park, NY: New City Press, 2019), 13-25.

43 *Ibid.*, 22.

44 *Letter 93*, 1.

to catch him and tie him up?'[45] Those rescued from Donatism would be like those rescued from physical harm: 'But once he had recovered his health, he would obviously thank him more profusely to the extent that he had felt that the man had spared him the less.'[46]

While the Old Testament pictures force being used against God's enemies, Augustine is happy to grant that such use of force is *not* to be found in the New Testament. However, in a very interesting move, Augustine turns to Psalm 2 and suggests that the prophecy of Psalm 2—where kings are called to serve the one true King—is being fulfilled in Augustine's own time. He writes:

> But this prophecy was not yet fulfilled: *And now, kings, have understanding; you who judge the earth, be warned; serve the Lord in fear* (Ps. 2:10-11). For what is said a little before in the same psalm was still being fulfilled, *Why have the nations raged and the people plotted in vain? The kings of earth have arisen, and the princes have gathered together against the Lord and against his anointed one* (Ps. 2:1-2).[47]

Augustine writes:

> [N]ow there is being fulfilled what is symbolized a little later by the same king when, after having been converted to honor the true God, he decreed in his kingdom that whoever blasphemed against the God of Shadrach, Meshach, and Abednego would face appropriate punishments. The earlier time of that king, therefore, signified the earlier times of non-believing kings, under whom the Christians suffered instead of the unbelievers, but the later time of that king signified the times of the later kings, who were now believers under whom the non-believers suffered instead of the Christians.[48]

---

45   *Ibid.*, 2.

46   *Ibid.*

47   *Ibid.*, 9.

48   *Ibid.* Augustine is referencing Daniel 3:29-30.

Augustine admits he has changed his mind on the use of force: 'For my opinion originally was that no one should be forced to the unity of Christ, but that we should act with words, fight with arguments, and conquer by reason.'[49] The main reason Augustine says he changed his mind was that he had seen the good results of the use of force—people returning to the Catholic Church (and this in his own city of Thagaste).[50] He could eventually say: 'Whoever is not found within the Church, is not to be asked why, but either he is to be corrected and converted or, if brought to book, let him not complain.'[51]

Augustine's doctrine of the Church and sacraments, and his engagement with Donatism, is endlessly fascinating. Augustine certainly sowed the seeds of the Roman Catholic system. The more one lingers on the implications of Augustine's writings on the Church and sacraments, the more one will see that much of later Church history can be read as attempts to follow Augustine, break from his influence, or significantly rework the thought of the Doctrine of Grace.

---

49   *Ibid.*, 17.

50   *Ibid.* Many of the arguments in *Letter 93* are also found in *Letter 185*, which Augustine in his *Reconsiderations* (2.48) renames *The Correction of the Donatists.*

51   *Against the Letters of Petilianus* 2.85. Quoted in Frend, *The Donatist Church*, 241.

7

AUGUSTINE, THE BIBLE, AND THE NATURE OF KNOWLEDGE AND LEARNING

Augustine and the Bible

The Nature and Authority of Scripture

Augustine gives ample testimony throughout his writings of his high view of Scripture. He is, of course, aware of various linguistic and translation issues (see especially *On Christian Doctrine*). Augustine would have worked mainly from the *Vetus Latina*—the 'Old Latin' translations. These were Latin texts derived from the Septuagint, which was a translation of the Hebrew Bible into Greek around 200 years before Christ.[1] For use in the churches, he prefers this Latin version of the Scriptures, in part because it is familiar to the congregants. However, he acknowledges that with the Old Testament, one should return to the Septuagint when necessary to handle various textual issues. He writes:

> Among the versions themselves, however, the *Itala* [i.e., the 'Old Latin'] is to be preferred to the rest, because it sticks more closely to the actual words, while at the same time having a clear perception of the meaning. And for correcting any Latin versions at all, Greek ones should be employed, among which,

---

1   Cf. Carol Harrison, 'Augustine,' in *The New Cambridge History of the Bible*, vol. 1, *From the Beginnings to 600* (Cambridge: Cambridge University Press, 2013), 677.

as regards the Old Testament, that of the Seventy Translators has the greatest authority.[2]

Augustine often speaks of the divine origin, inspiration, and authority of Scripture. In *The City of God*, he writes of Christ, the Holy Spirit, and the Scriptures as follows:

> This Mediator, having spoken what He judged sufficient, first by the prophets, then by His own lips, and afterwards by the apostles, has besides produced the Scripture which is called canonical, which has paramount authority, and to which we yield assent in all matters of which we ought not to be ignorant, and yet cannot know of ourselves.[3]

In the same letter (*Letter 83*, to Jerome), Augustine writes, 'I most firmly believe that none of their authors erred in writing anything.'[4] Augustine also argues that one should not dispute that the Bible is free from error: 'With regard to their writings [i.e., the writings of the prophets and the apostles] it is wicked to doubt that they are free from all error.'[5]

The Authority of Scripture and the Nature of the Church

Perhaps one of Augustine's most famous statements on how he came to believe Scripture is as follows: 'I would not believe the holy Gospels if it were not for the authority of the Holy Catholic Church.'[6] While it might be tempting to some to take this passage as sure-fire support for some sort of two-source view of divine authority (i.e., Scripture and the Roman Catholic Church/Petrine authority), or as a proof-text of sorts for papal infallibility, other passages in Augustine mitigate against such a move. For example, it is clear that Augustine looks to the

---

2   *On Christian Doctrine* II.15.22.

3   *City of God* XI.2.

4   *Letter 82 (from Augustine to Jerome)* 3.

5   *Ibid.*, 1.3.

6   *Against the 'Foundation Letter' of the Manichees* 5.6.

Scriptures as his ultimate authority, giving evidence (at the risk of being anachronistic) of a version of 'sola scriptura.' He writes: 'I owe this complete obedience only to the canonical Scriptures, and by it I follow them alone in such a way that I have no doubt that their authors erred in them in absolutely no way and wrote nothing in them in order to deceive.'[7]

Likewise Augustine can speak of the 'lofty supremacy' and authority of Scripture, and of Scripture's ultimate authority in relation to what follows subsequently in church history: 'There is a distinct boundary line separating all productions subsequent to apostolic times from the authoritative canonical books of the Old and New Testaments. The authority of these books has come down to us from the apostles through the successions of bishops and the extension of the Church, and, from a position of lofty supremacy, claims the submission of every faithful and pious mind.'[8] Indeed, the Scriptures rightly demand an obedience due to their 'distinctive peculiarity': '[I]n consequence of the distinctive peculiarity of the sacred writings, we are bound to receive as true whatever the canon shows to have been said by even one prophet, or apostle, or evangelist.'[9]

The Unity of Holy Scripture

Augustine is at a number of points concerned to maintain the fundamental unity of Holy Scripture. Augustine writes: 'The words they hated to see ascribed to God in the Old Testament were righteous enough to be found in the New, and those they praised and celebrated in the New Testament were also to be found in the Old.'[10] Similarly, Augustine writes: '[Among the

---

7   *Letter 82 (from Augustine to Jerome)* 3.24.

8   *Contra Faustum, a Manichee* 5.

9   *Ibid.*

10   *Contra Adimantum* IV. This work is *Against Adimantus* ('Adimantum' is just the Latin direct object form of 'Adimantus'). The 'they' in this work is the Manichees. Adimantus was a Manichee. The Manichees would have been less friendly to the Old Testament, in which God 'gets His hands dirty' with creation. Augustine,

people who had received the Old Testament] there were so many signs and such preparation for the New Testament that we can find in the Gospel and the apostles' preaching no precept, no promise, however difficult and divine they may be, that is missing from those ancient books.'[11] In affirming the unity of the Bible Augustine writes: 'The meaning of the New Testament lies hidden in the Old, the meaning of the Old Testament is revealed through the New.'[12]

The Interpretation of Scripture

Augustine exhibits several approaches to Scripture as he interprets it in apologetic and pastoral contexts. He consistently is interested in what we today call 'authorial intent.' He is focused first and foremost on the divine author of Scripture: in reading the Bible, Christians are attempting to discover and discern the mind of God. Augustine writes that readers of Scripture are attempting 'to discover the thoughts and will of the authors it was written by, and through them to discover the will of God, which we believe directed what such human writers had to say.'[13]

At numerous points Augustine points his readers to the necessity of approaching Scripture with certain expectations, especially when it comes to making sense of the difficult passages. Augustine says that there are 'secrets' (mysteries or things difficult to understand) that God has placed in Scripture on purpose to arouse our desire to search the Scriptures. Augustine is also quite clear that God has *intentionally* made Scripture difficult to understand, so that we must *work* at understanding Scripture:

---

having left Manicheeism, is eager to show that the God of the Old Testament is the same God as the God of the New Testament. So, he is here attempting to show a fundamental unity between the words of the Old Testament and the words of the New Testament.

11   *Contra Adimantum* III.4.

12   *On the Instruction of Beginners* IV.8.

13   *On Christian Doctrine* II.6.7.

[The difficulty of understanding and interpreting Scripture] is all due, I have no doubt at all, to divine providence, in order to break in pride with hard labor, and to save the intelligence from boredom, since it readily forms a low opinion of things that are too easy to work out.[14]

Augustine also writes about his former efforts to approach Scripture from an unbelieving heart. No one who is unbelieving can rightly interpret Scripture:

[I]f you have no qualms about believing, there's nothing you need be ashamed of. I am speaking to you as one who was myself caught out once upon a time, when as a lad I wanted to tackle the divine Scriptures with the techniques of clever disputation before bringing to them the spirit of earnest inquiry. In this way I was shutting the door of my Lord against myself by my misplaced attitude; I should have been knocking at it for it to be opened, but instead I was adding my weight to keep it shut. I was presuming to seek in my pride what can only be found by humility.[15]

Interpreting Scripture is not easy, and Augustine closes *Sermon 51* with the following words:

If any of you is eager for more, you must knock at the door of the one from whom I too have received what I have been able to grasp and to express. Above all, don't forget this: not to be unduly troubled when you don't yet understand the holy Scriptures; when you do understand them, not to get a swollen head. Instead, respectfully put to one side anything you don't understand, and anything you do understand hold firmly to in a spirit of love.[16]

Like many Christians of his day, Augustine affirmed that one could seek four types of meaning in Scripture:

---

14   *Ibid.*

15   *Sermon* 51.6.

16   *Ibid.*, 51.35.

1. Historical (the plain sense)
2. Allegorical (the figurative meaning)
3. Analogical (dealing with harmony of old and new covenants)
4. Aetiological (dealing with the origin or cause of things)[17]

He summarizes these four levels as follows:

> Four ways of expounding the law have been laid down by
> some Scripture commentators, which can be named in words
> derived from the Greek, while they need further definition and
> explanation in plain Latin; they are the way of history, the way
> of allegory, the way of analogy, the way of aetiology. History is
> when things done by God or man are recounted; allegory when
> they are understood as being said figuratively; analogy, when the
> harmony of the old and new covenants is being demonstrated;
> aetiology, when the causes of the things that have been said and
> done are presented.[18]

---

17 It can be a tad confusing, for later medieval thinkers will speak of a 'fourfold sense,'
but speak of a different four senses! Thomas Aquinas speaks of the following
four senses: (1) literal, (2) allegorical, (3) tropological, and (4) anagogical. One
commentator notes: 'To be added here is what Augustine says in *The Advantage of
Believing* 3 (PL 42:68) and Saint Thomas cites in *Summa theologica* i, q. 1, a. 10, as
follows: "Scripture which is entitled the Old Testament has a fourfold meaning,
namely according to history, to etiology, to analogy, to allegory." Saint Thomas
does not regard this as a valid objection to his own fourfold division into the
literal, allegorical, tropological, and anagogical senses, and he comments as follows
on Augustine: "These three, history, etiology, and analogy, are grouped under
the one general heading of the literal sense. For as Saint Augustine explains in
the same place, you have history when any matter is straightforwardly recorded;
etiology when its cause is indicated, as when our Lord pointed to men's hardness
of heart as the reason why Moses allowed them to set aside their wives; analogy
when the truth of one scriptural passage is shown not to clash with the truth of
another. Of the four senses enumerated in the argument, allegory stands alone for
the three spiritual senses of our exposition"' (*Summa theologiae* I. *Christian Theology*
[Ia, I], trans. T. Gilby [New York, 1964] 37, 39). This insight and quotation on
the difference between Augustine and Thomas is found in footnote 61 of Prosper
Grech's 'Hermeneutical Principles of Saint Augustine in *Teaching Christianity*,' in
Teaching Christianity, 94.

18 *Unfinished Literal Commentary on Genesis 2.*

Augustine's love for Scripture goes beyond his desire to understand it. Sometimes, it simply results in poetry: 'To myself I was death. In you I am recovering life. Speak to me, instruct me, I have put faith in your books. And their words are mysteries indeed.'[19]

The faith Augustine puts in 'the books' is worth exploring. How can we know that we are interpreting them rightly? Augustine contends that Jesus' teaching about the greatest commandment should guide our thinking about how to interpret the Bible. The passage Augustine refers to (Matt. 22:37–40) says:

> You shall love the Lord your God with all your heart and with all your soul and with all your mind. This is the great and first commandment. And a second is like it: You shall love your neighbor as yourself. On these two commandments depend all the Law and the Prophets.

Augustine comments, in light of this passage: 'So what difficulty is it for me when these words [of Genesis] can be interpreted in various ways, provided only that the interpretations are true?'[20] It *appears* that Augustine's position is: as long as an interpretation advances love of God and love of neighbor, or perhaps is consistent with these two loves, that interpretation is true. He says that an interpreter can arrive at a conclusion that God Himself would grant as true, *even if* this interpretation is not the meaning intended by the author:

> As long as each interpreter is endeavouring to find in the Holy Scriptures the meaning of the author who wrote it, what evil is it if an exegesis he gives is one shown to be true by you, light of all sincere souls, even if the author whom he is reading did not have that idea and, though he had grasped a truth, had not discerned that seen by the interpreter?[21]

---

19. *Confessions* XII.10.10.

20 *Ibid.*, XII.18.27.

21 *Ibid.*

In light of these interpretive strategies, Augustine can work through, in a single work, *five* possible interpretations of both Genesis 1:1 ('In the beginning God created the heavens and the earth') and Genesis 1:2 ('The earth was without form and void, and darkness was over the face of the deep').[22] After these options Augustine makes an important distinction between (1) 'the *truth* of the matter in question,' and (2) 'the *intention* of the writer.'[23] Augustine is quite clear that God has spoken clearly through His servant: 'I would approach the words of your book to seek in them your will through the intention of your servant, by whose pen you imparted them to us.'[24] But when it comes to trying to state clearly what the author (in the case of Genesis for Augustine, Moses) meant, Augustine is a bit cautious. There are multiple interpretations which might be *true* in the *theological* sense. But Augustine (and other interpreters) might struggle to get right exactly what the author (again, here Moses) intended. At the same time, every Christian should affirm that *whatever* Moses did actually intend, what his writing intends to communicate must be true.[25]

Augustine in the end is not sure what view on Genesis 1:1-2 was held by Moses, but he does assert that multiple interpretations could be true in the larger theological sense.[26] And indeed, in *another* sense Moses intended 'that meaning which supremely corresponds both to the light of truth and to the reader's spiritual profit.'[27] Indeed, Augustine suggests that

22   *Ibid.*, XII.20.29–21.30. Though Augustine grants the theological difficulty of options that would posit in any way that there was some thing there before creation that was 'formless' and 'void.'

23   *Ibid.*, XII.23.32.

24   *Ibid.*

25   *Ibid.* XII.24.33 and XII.25.35. 'Moses meant whatever he meant in those books. If we do not believe, we make the Lord a liar ...' (XII.24.35).

26   *Ibid.* XII.30.41.

27   *Ibid.*

Moses 'intended' numerous interpretations.[28] This approach is partially an outworking of Augustine's stance of humility toward Scripture. He does not want to presume that he knows what is in Moses' or God's mind.

In the last book of *Confessions*, Augustine often speaks poetically about the nature and authority of Scripture. Thus Augustine can write: 'Who but you, O God, has made for us a solid firmament of authority over us in your divine Scripture?'[29] Indeed, 'Preachers of your word pass from this life to another life, but your Scripture is "stretched out" over the peoples to the end of the age.'[30] For the angels, at least, God Himself is a kind of book: 'They ever read, and what they read never passes away. By choosing and loving they read the immutability of your desiring. Their codex is never closed, nor is their book ever folded shut.'[31]

Augustine is quite happy to admit that sometimes we simply do not know how to make sense of this or that Scripture. Nonetheless, the believer still affirms that Scripture is true. Augustine writes:

> We submit our intellect to [Scripture], and hold for certain that even language closed to our comprehension is right and true. Even a person who is spiritual and is 'renewed in the knowledge of God according to the image of him who created him' (Col. 3:10) has to be a 'doer of the law' (James 4:11), not its critic.[32]

Part of what makes Scripture so thoroughly special and unique is that Scripture is a word which comes to us *in time*, but God Himself is *outside of time*. Thus, Augustine puts the following

---

28   *Ibid.* But see the next section (43), where Augustine seems to qualify this a bit.

29   *Ibid.* XIII.25.16. Referencing Isa. 34:4.

30   *Ibid.* XIII.25.18. Referencing Matt. 24:35.

31   *Ibid.*

32   *Ibid.* XIII.23.33.

words in the mouth of God Himself: 'O man, what my Scripture says, I say.' Then Augustine has God go on to say:

> So, I see those things which through my Spirit you see, just as I also say the things which through my Spirit you say. Accordingly, while your [i.e., man's] vision of them is temporally determined, my seeing is not temporal, just as you speak of these things in temporal terms but I do not speak in the successiveness of time.[33]

Illumination, Knowing, the Liberal Arts, and Words and Things

Illumination and How One Knows

Augustine has a lot to say about how we know. This is an important theme, for it is here that Thomas Aquinas departs from Augustine in interesting ways (more on that later). The question of how one knows is a classic question in Western thought. The technical term is 'epistemology' (*'epistēmē'* is one Greek word for 'knowledge,' and *'logos'* is the Greek word for 'word,' or can have the sense of 'study'). In broad strokes what separates Augustine from our own day is that today, at least in the dominant secular understanding, one thinks about the nature of knowledge without any reference to God. For Augustine (and for virtually any traditional Christian thinker), one construes the nature of knowing with at least *some* reference to God.

In his work *The Teacher*, Augustine asks how we know that this or that 'sign' refers to this or that 'thing' (Augustine speaks of 'signs' and 'things' often, especially in *On Christian Doctrine*). In a dialogue between himself and Adeodatus (his son's name), Augustine probes the question of how we know that a sign refers to a thing, and—ultimately—how we know at all. In the midst of this discussion Augustine makes a striking assertion: a teacher

---

33   *Ibid.* XIII.29.44.

really does *not* 'teach' his students anything. Rather, the teacher speaks or teaches, and as he does so, the student looks within and discovers the truth. But it is a truth which the student—in a sense—already possesses.

In trying to grasp what Augustine says about illumination, it is helpful to get some key texts in front of us. This material can be a bit dense. As we will see as we unpack things a bit, there are several issues at work here:

1. God is at work somehow assisting/allowing/making possible/etc., human knowing.
2. It truly is the *human person* who knows—that is, God's knowing does not in any way replace or undermine human knowing.
3. God has created or structured man as a knowing creature.
4. God has created or structured the world such that it is knowable.
5. There is an *uncreated* 'light' (God) and the *created* light of the human intellect—and God so works in knowing that there is real relation between these two lights.

Here is Augustine on knowing:

> But the light itself [that illuminates our knowing] is something else [than what is known], the light by which the soul is enlightened in order truly to understand and observe all things either in itself or in this light. For this light is now God Himself, while the soul is a creature, even though a rational and intelligent one made to His image. So when it strives to gaze upon that light, it blinks and shivers in its weakness, and quite simply lacks the power to do so. Yet that light is what enables it to understand *whatever is within the range of its power.* When therefore it is snatched up there, and being withdrawn from the senses of the flesh is set more firmly in the presence of that vision, not spatially but in its own kind of way, it also sees above

itself the one by whose aid it also is enabled to see whatever it can see in itself by intellectual understanding.[34]

One of the things Augustine is doing here is distinguishing (1) seeing the light itself (which is God), from (2) things we see *in the light of that* light. So 'that light' (God) is 'what enables us to understand *whatever is within the range of its power.*' Augustine is here reflecting on 1 Corinthians 13:12, where Paul speaks of a face-to-face vision of God. Thus, when Augustine (in the quote above) speaks of being 'snatched up there,' he appears to be speaking of such a face-to-face vision (which Paul may have gotten a small glimpse of in his life, but which ultimately is a future reality for Christians). For our purposes here, it is important to note that, at least here in his writings, Augustine seems to teach that it is the 'light' (i.e., God) who illumines the human mind in every act of knowing—i.e., allows understanding of '*whatever is within its range of power.*'

But also note the final sentence of this quotation: 'It also sees above itself the one by whose aid it also is enabled to see whatever it can see *in itself* by intellectual understanding' (emphasis mine). Note how Augustine speaks of what one can see 'in itself' (or in oneself). There is a recurring note in Augustine: we come to understand things by—in some sense—looking *within*. This will get pushed in a certain direction by Bonaventure (influenced by Francis of Assisi), and—we might say—will get secularized or even 'naturalized' in unique ways by Descartes (the seventeenth-century French philosopher).[35]

Let's look at few other key texts which speak of illumination. Here is Augustine from *The Trinity* 12.15.24:

---

34   *Literal Interpretation of Genesis* XII.31.59. Emphasis mine. This is pretty dense material. Ronald Nash wrote his doctoral dissertation on the concept of illumination in Augustine. See below for my attempt to boil this down to a simple summary.

35   I am working on a monograph tentatively titled *This is Eternal Life: A Biblical Theology of Knowledge* where I try to work some of these ideas out in greater detail.

[T]he nature of the intellectual mind has been so established by the disposition of its creator that it is subjoined to intelligible things in the order of nature, and so it sees such truths in a kind of non-bodily light that is *sui generis* [i.e., unique], just as our eyes of flesh see all these things that lie around us in this bodily light, a light they were created to be receptive of and to match.

Notice two things in this passage that must be held together if we are to make sense of Augustine. Our intellectual mind is such that we are created or structured with the *capacity*[36] to know things. It is *also* the case that when we know things we see in 'a kind of non-bodily light,' a light that is *unique (sui generis)*—and this light is God. That is, Augustine is able to affirm: (1) we are created/structured to know, and (2) it is God who illumines the mind to make knowledge possible.[37]

---

36   When I speak of 'capacity,' this should be distinguished from the question of 'ability.' By 'capacity' I simply mean that when God created persons, persons were structured to know God. 'Capacity' does not entail 'autonomy' or 'autonomous ability to know God,' or the like.

37   I do not want to push texts beyond what they can bear, but a point should be made. I found over the years that in theology one of the toughest things for persons to hold together is related to divine and human agency. In theology we are dealing with *God*, but we are also dealing with *how God and creation relate*. In much of theology we are wrestling with how to understand this relationship (in its varied ways) between God and man. When we are thinking about the possibility and reality of knowledge (at least here in Augustine's attempt to make sense of the issue), we are dealing with this perennial issue. Augustine is able to hold two things together which many Christian thinkers desire to tear asunder: (1) As *created* beings, we have certain created capacities or structures that make knowledge possible (think here in terms of *human agency*—we are the ones who know things); (2) it is God who illumines the mind, or—as the Light—brings about knowledge in the human knower (think here in terms of *divine agency*). As I see it, *Thomism*—at least in certain forms or construals—desires to so 'privilege' the human knower as to make divine illumination unnecessary (of 'natural' things). On the other hand, a more *Franciscan* understanding desires to 'privilege' God's place in the knowing process by contending that God somehow 'impresses' the thoughts or knowledge in the mind of the human knower. Augustine—with a robust affirmation of both human and divine agency—is able to hold these things together.

Let us also turn to *Soliloquies*.[38] In I.1.3. Augustine writes of 'God, the intelligible light, in whom and from whom and through whom all things intelligibly shine, which anywhere intelligibly shine.' And in I.8.15 Augustine, speaking of God and the possibility of knowledge, can say:

> Namely, God is intelligible, not sensible, intelligible also are those demonstrations of the schools; nevertheless they differ very widely. For as the earth is visible, so is light; but the earth, unless illumined by light, cannot be seen. Therefore those things also which are taught in the schools, which no one who understands them doubts in the least to be absolutely true, we must believe to be incapable of being understood, unless they are illuminated by somewhat else, as it were a sun of their own.[39]

He continues:

> Therefore as in this visible sun we may observe three things: [1] that he is, [2] that he shines, [3] that he illuminates: so in that God most far withdrawn whom thou wouldst fain apprehend, there are these three things: [1] that He is, [2] that He is apprehended, and [3] that He makes other things to be apprehended.[40]

Augustine also deals with illumination in *The Trinity*. He writes:

> Our enlightenment is to participate in the Word, that is, in that *life which is the light of men* (John 1:4). Yet we were absolutely incapable of such participation and quite unfit for it, so unclean were we through sin, so we had to be cleansed....By nature we are not God; by nature we are men; by sin we are not just. So God became a just man to intercede with God for sinful man.

---

38   I am working here from *Nicene and Post-Nicene Fathers*, volume 7, *Augustine: Homilies on the Gospel of John, Homilies on the First Epistle of John, Soliloquies*, edited by Philip Schaff (Peabody, Massachusetts: Hendrickson Publishers, 1994).

39   *Soliloquies* I.8.15.

40   My enumeration.

But equally importantly, we see in this quotation from *The Trinity* a theme that is seen consistently throughout this key work: We need the atoning blood of Christ to purify and cleanse us, so that we might be fit to one day see God face-to-face. And so, 'the only thing to cleanse the wicked and the proud is the blood of the just man and the humility of God; to contemplate God, which by nature we are not, we would have to be cleansed by Him who became what by nature we are and what by sin we are not.'

Augustine also touches on illumination in *The Trinity*. He writes:

> [T]he more brightly burns our love for God, the more surely and serenely we see Him, because it is in God that we observe that unchanging form of justice which we judge that a man should live up to. Faith therefore is a great help for knowing and loving God, not as though He were altogether unknown or altogether not loved without it, but for knowing Him all the more clearly and loving Him all the more firmly.[41]

There are a couple of important aspects of Augustine's theology here. First, note the link Augustine makes between (1) our love for God, and (2) our ability to see Him: '... the more brightly burns our love for God, the more surely and serenely we see him.' For Augustine, as for many Christian thinkers, our ability to *know* or 'see' God is linked to the state of our hearts—whether we truly love God or not.[42] Second, note that it is 'in God' that persons 'observe that unchanging form of justice.' Somehow,

---

41   *The Trinity* 8.9.13.

42   Again, when turning inward gets pressed (perhaps too far), we can end up with a hyper-Bonaventurism—where we turn 'inward' in such a way, and this turn inward in a sense *remains* and *stays* inward. For Augustine, at least at his best, the turn inward allowed us to know more fully a real world (and a real God) who exists outside of us. This inward turn, when radicalized, or indeed one might say when it becomes perverted, can lead (and this is a generalization) to Descartes. I do *not* mean to say that Augustine leads to Descartes. I mean to say that Augustine's turn inward must be seen in light of the reality that all knowing is 'in God,' and it is God who illumines the mind and undergirds all knowledge, and who makes

for Augustine, when we know, we are knowing 'in God.' Our knowledge is possible because it takes place in God.

In *Confessions* Augustine writes: 'If we both see that what you say is true, and we both see that what I say is true, where do we see it? I certainly do not see it in you, nor do you in me; we both see it in the immutable truth itself which towers above our minds.'[43] Here Augustine affirms that two persons agree on the truth, but 'where' does one see it? Ultimately, for Augustine, both persons 'see' it in God Himself—'the immutable truth itself which towers above our minds.'

But let us look a bit more at what Augustine actually says. In *Sermon* 67.8 Augustine writes:

> Say that you are not your own light. At the most you are an eye; you are not light. What's the use of an open and healthy eye, if there's no light? So say it; you don't get any light from yourself, and cry out what is written, *You will light my lamp, O Lord*; with your light, Lord, *you will light up my darkness* (Ps. 18:28). I mean, all I have is darkness; you are the light dispelling the darkness, lighting up me; it's not from me that light comes to me, but the only original, uncreated light is in you.[44]

So, we are not our *own* light. There is a need for an *uncreated* light—God—if I am going to know things.

In *Contra Faustum* 20.7 Augustine explicitly speaks of an 'uncreated light' (which is God the Trinity), and a created light (which is we, or our knowing capacity). As Augustine writes:

> And yet even this light is not the light which is God, for this light is a creature, whereas that light is the creator. This light was made, whereas that light is its maker. This light, finally, is mutable, since it wills what it used not to will and knows what it used not to know and remembers what was forgotten, but that

---

knowing possible. Descartes' 'inward turn' *in effect* leaves God outside of the knowing process.

43   *Confessions* 12.25.35.

44   *Sermon* 67.8.

light remains with an immutable will, truth, and eternity, and from it we have the beginning of our existence, the basis of our knowing, and the law of our loving.... That light, then, is the undivided Trinity, the one God.[45]

The most important biblical passage speaking, it seems, *directly* to the question of illumination, is John 1:9. Augustine's comments are intriguing and are consonant with the views discussed above:

> Hence, the gospel says, *He was the true light that enlightens every human being that comes into this world* (John 1:9). The gospel said this, because no human being is enlightened save by that light of the truth which is God. Thus none should suppose that they are enlightened so as to learn by someone from whom they hear something. And I do not mean merely if one happens to have as a teacher some great human being, but not even if one happens to have an angel. The word of truth is externally presented by means of a bodily voice; nonetheless, *neither the one who plants nor the one who waters is anything; it is, rather, God who gives the increase* (1 Cor. 3:7). A human being hears someone speaking, either another human being or an angel, but in order that one might see and know that what is said is true, that light which remains eternally, but also *shines in the darkness* (John 1:5), is interiorly shed upon the mind. But as this sun in our sky is not seen by the blind, though it in a sense clothes them with its rays, so this light is not grasped by the darkness of folly.[46]

Augustine's reflections on the nature of human knowing can be rather dense and difficult. Here is an abbreviated outline of the key issues.

Three Key Summative Points:
1. God is light and illumines all humans to different degrees.
2. There are intelligible truths, the *rationes aeternae* ('eternal reasons'), which God illumines.

---

45 *Contra Faustum* XX.7.

46 *The Punishment and Forgiveness of Sins and the Baptism of Little Ones* XXIV.37.

3. Human minds can know the divine truths only as God illumines them.

Concerning Knowledge:
• The ideas in the mind are *a priori*, virtual preconditions of scientia ('knowledge')
   → *A priori*: cannot be derived from experience.
   → *Virtual*: These ideas are in the mind even when they are not objects of thought.
   → Knowledge becomes possible only when these universals are applied to images from sensation.

Concerning Man:
• Man is endowed with a structure of rationality patterned after the divine ideas in God's own mind.
• There are two 'lights': (1) uncreated light of God; (2) created, mutable light of the human intellect; God so works in knowing that there is real relation between these two lights.
• Humans can know the truth because God has made us like Himself (in the *imago Dei*).
• Humans can know the *corporeal* world because we first know and understand the *intelligible* world.
• Humans possess as part of our nature forms of thought by which man knows and judges sensible things.

Thus, we are both (1) structured such that knowledge is possible, and (2) there is the constant, immanent, active presence of God allowing knowledge to occur.[47]

---

47 Ronald Nash wrote his doctoral dissertation on Augustine's understanding of human knowing. His work is published as *The Light of the Mind: St. Augustine's Theory of Knowledge* (Lexington: University of Kentucky Press, 1969). This is still the seminal work in the field. Nash has condensed this material into the 'Illumination' entry in *Augustine Through the Ages*. I strongly recommend that readers take a look at the *Augustine Through the Ages* entry as a way into these issues. I have created a one-page chart that I have posted at www.bradleyggreen.com. My summary here is a condensation to some degree of the *Augustine Through the Ages* entry.

Augustine and the Liberal Arts

Augustine holds a venerable place in the Western tradition of thinking about the nature of education, of learning, and, in particular, of the liberal arts. Indeed, Augustine desired to write treatises on all of the traditional liberal arts.[48] Unfortunately, all we have from his pen are the works On Grammar and On Music, and perhaps one on dialectic.[49] But perhaps most important for Christians in our day is that Augustine is eagerly focused on how Christians should construe the educational or learning task. To generalize a bit, much of Western educational practice can be understood in terms of how one does or does not develop Augustine's desire to construe an explicitly Christian path or plan for the educational endeavor.[50]

Augustine looked back on his education with some lament and even disdain. He reports that his teachers taught grammar, dialectic, and rhetoric, but were not concerned with his moral and spiritual formation. He observes: 'See the exact care with which the sons of men observe the conventions of letters and syllables received from those who so talked before them.' But, Augustine continues: 'Yet they neglect the eternal contracts of lasting salvation received from you.'[51] Like Paul in 1 Corinthians 2, Augustine was aware that rhetoric (one can think simply of the use of words in general here) could be used to mislead and even abuse people. Indeed, Augustine is quite negative about the 'the school of loquacious chattering,' that is, with people who use words in a way dislocated from truth and love.[52]

---

48 *Reconsiderations* 1.6.

49 There is some dispute as to whether the book we possess on dialectic is from Augustine's pen. According to Boniface Ramsey, the scholarly consensus is that the work on dialectic is in fact from Augustine himself. Cf. *Reconsiderations* 1.6 (note 75).

50 There are of course other Christians, indeed early in church history, who gave sustained attention to the nature of learning and education.

51 *Confessions* I.18.29.

52 *Ibid.* VIII.5.10.

For Augustine the liberal arts are good things, as are one's intellectual gifts to use or exercise the arts. But the liberal arts and one's intellectual gifts must ultimately be offered back to God. Augustine writes that he enjoyed the liberal arts, 'not recognizing the source of whatever elements of truth and certainty they contained.'[53] Augustine's intellectual gifts should have been offered to God: 'Yet from this gift I offered you no sacrifice. It therefore worked not to my advantage but rather to my harm, because I took care that this excellent part of my substance should be under my own control, and I did not guard my strength by approaching you, but left you and set out for a distant land to squander it there on the quest for meretricious gratifications.'[54] Indeed: 'What profit was this good gift to me when I failed to use it well?' And because Augustine did not grasp that intellectual gifts and capacities are *gifts*:

> It only made me less able to appreciate how very difficult these liberal arts were for even the most zealous and clever to understand. I found this out only when I tried to expound them to my pupils, among whom only the brightest could follow my explanation without dragging.[55]

Even though it will be worked out and developed more fully later in the course of church history, Augustine bequeaths to the West the beginnings of an attempt to work out an explicitly Christian theological framework for the life of the mind and for learning. Similarly, Augustine was the first Christian to give *extended* attention to a related issue—the nature of words and signs, to which we now turn.

---

53 *Ibid.* IV.16.30.

54 *Ibid.*

55 *Ibid.*

Augustine on Words, Signs, and Things

It is interesting that in Umberto Eco's book on semiotics he jumps from the ancient Greeks directly to Augustine.[56] In the first five centuries of the church's life, Augustine is the first Christian thinker to give sustained attention to the nature of words and signs. He articulates, in a sense, his own Christian theory, or even theology, of language. From *The Teacher, On Christian Teaching,* and *The Trinity,* one can forge an impressive incarnational theory of language. And it is not naïve in the least. Augustine does affirm that words have meaning and have the ability to signify something. And as one explores his understanding of language, one is quickly led into his epistemology, for questions of meaning and knowledge quickly emerge as one focuses on the nature of language.

Although Augustine speaks to the nature of language at a number of different points in his corpus, we can gain insight to his way of thinking by looking briefly at *The Teacher* and *On Christian Doctrine.* Thus, in *On Christian Doctrine* Augustine notes that there are 'signs' and 'things.'[57] 'Signs' point to 'things,' and signs are *also* things. And there is *one* ultimate 'thing'—God.

Augustine states that 'all teaching is either about things or signs.'[58] Signs 'are used to signify something else.'[59] Words are one kind of sign, but not the only kind. In addition, signs are also 'things,' because if 'signs' were not also 'things,' 'signs' would be nothing. But this does not mean that every 'thing' is a 'sign.' In short, every 'sign' is a 'thing,' but not every 'thing' is a 'sign.'

---

56   In his discussion and survey of 'signs,' Umberto Eco moves from the Stoics' reflection on such issues to Augustine's thought on these same issues. See his work, *Semiotics and the Philosophy of Language* (Bloomington, IN: Indiana University Press, 1984), 33-35.

57   *On Christian Doctrine* I.

58   *Ibid.* I.2.2.

59   *Ibid.*

'Things' are to be either 'used' or 'enjoyed,' depending on what kind of thing they are. The Triune God ('one supreme thing') is to be 'enjoyed,' while all other things are to be 'used.'[60] That is, all other 'things' are instruments to be used on one's journey to God (the 'supreme thing').[61] God is inexpressible, but yet even to say God is inexpressible *is* to say something about God.[62] Augustine recognizes this dilemma, and posits that God still 'accepts' human words directed at Him: God 'has accepted the homage of human voices, and has wished us to rejoice in praising him with our words.'[63] For Augustine language can be limited, but still be useful and even adequate.

For Augustine there are seven realities or stages,[64] and a person moves from one to another in something like a sequence: fear of God (stage 1) leads to piety (stage 2), both of which are necessary for knowledge (stage 3). A person then moves to fortitude or courage (stage 4), mercy (stage 5), and the purging and cleaning of the eyes (stage 6), and all of this culminates in wisdom (stage 7). For those of us who are Protestants, we cannot help but see in Augustine's discussion of these stages a conceptual link to Calvin's understanding of the two-fold knowledge of God (knowledge of God and knowledge of self), as found in the opening pages of the *Institutes*.

A Protestant Reflection

At times Protestants—at least conservative Protestants—are accused of being modernists, rationalists, de facto secularists, and

---

60 *Ibid.* I.5.5; I.22.20.

61 David Lyle Jeffrey notes: 'For Augustine even a theory of signs is therefore ultimately based on considerations of intention and the ordering of value.' That is, Augustine's theory of signs is rooted in his ethical views, which are part of Augustine's larger Christian vision. See Jeffrey, *People of the Book: Christian Identity and Literary Culture* (Grand Rapids: Eerdmans, 1996), 83.

62 *On Christian Doctrine* I.6.6.

63 *Ibid.*

64 *Ibid.* II.9–11.

more whenever we articulate a doctrine of the full inspiration, authority, and inerrancy of Holy Scripture. Certainly any and every group wants to be open to criticism, and to be open to hearing words that might help remove blinders and sharpen one's thinking. But it is interesting to note that Augustine's fundamental concerns about how we should approach Scripture appear in various Protestant thinkers—although it is a different question as to whether this or that Protestant thinker is self-consciously relying on Augustine.

Thus, for example, the Old Princetonians can consistently and repeatedly argue that it is only 'right reason' which can truly operate as reason *ought* to operate. That is, the Old Princetonians affirm the importance of reason, but consistently argue that it is only 'right reason' which can properly function as 'reason.' It is only when the person is properly related to the risen Lord Jesus that one's reason works rightly—particularly in relation to interpreting Scripture correctly.[65]

With Augustine, to truly have knowledge of God means that our knowing process must be shaped and formed by the reality of the God of Scripture at all points. That is: does Augustine's thought allow for an understanding of knowledge where knowledge is *at any point* autonomous, or even quasi-autonomous? And here we bump into a delicate issue. Thomas Aquinas argues that knowledge of the natural realm does *not*

---

65   On the Old Princetonians especially, see Paul Kjoss Helseth, *'Right Reason' and the Princeton Mind: An Unorthodox Proposal* (Phillipsburg, NJ: Presbyterian and Reformed Publishers, 2010). The question of the relationship between (1) rightly relating to Christ and (2) epistemological 'success' is a big question, one we deal with at greater length in the section on Augustine and illumination. Thomas Pfau has written that some of Augustine's insights in this area would actually resurface—in a sense—in the thought of Edmund Husserl (a twentieth-century philosopher, and the founder of 'Phenomenology'). Pfau notes: 'A person's "responsiveness" even to seemingly elemental, sensory phenomena invariably presupposes, and potentially reveals, her or his spiritual condition or will; all perception always implies (and potentially reveals) something qualitative about the percept and the perceiver.' See Thomas Pfau, *Minding the Modern: Human Agency, Intellectual Traditions, and Responsible Knowledge* (Notre Dame, IN: University of Notre Dame Press, 2013), 130.

require divine illumination, while knowledge of the supernatural realm *does* require divine illumination. In fairness to Thomas, he *does* say that God must *orchestrate* the entire knowing process. But nonetheless, *divine illumination* is *not* necessary when one knows natural (i.e., *non-*supernatural) things. One wonders: do Augustine's epistemological commitments find a more natural fulfillment in the Roman Catholic tradition, which is so thoroughly shaped by Thomas, or does the Augustinian trajectory ultimately find its more natural fulfillment in the Protestant tradition—particularly amongst the Reformed, a tradition which seems more fully committed to an Augustinian understanding of the nature of the knowing process?

In sum: Augustine offers a philosophy of signs that grounds our words in the Incarnate Word, and that directs our signs (words) to the ultimate thing, God—giving our language an eschatological focus and meaning. Words, language, and signs, for Augustine, are inherently tied to the nature and purposes of God. We can plunder from Augustine his formulation of a doctrine of words, language and signs in explicitly Christian and theological terms.

8

AUGUSTINE, CIVIL AUTHORITY, AND THE CITY OF GOD

Problems with the Pagans

The City of God is clearly Augustine's *magnum opus*. Filling 22 books and 867 pages in the English translation that is in front of me, it is one of the truly classic works of Western thought.[1] Augustine wrote *The City of God* from 413 to 427. In 410 Alaric and the Visigoths had successfully invaded Rome, and it seemed that Rome was no longer impenetrable.[2] Why was Rome susceptible to defeat? Augustine authors *The City of God*— in part—to counteract certain persons who wanted to blame Rome's adoption of the Christian faith for Rome's susceptibility. He says:

> The glorious city of God is my theme in this work .... I have undertaken its defense against those who prefer their own gods to the Founder of this city—a city surpassingly glorious, whether we view it as it still lives by faith in this fleeting course of time, and sojourns as a stranger in the midst of the ungodly, or as it shall dwell in the fixed stability of its eternal seat, which it now with patience waits for, expecting until 'righteousness shall

---

1   Augustine, *The City of God*, translated by Marcus Dods (New York: Modern Library, 1950).

2   Rome was not 'conquered' by the Visigoths, who withdrew after three days. Nonetheless, it now seemed that Rome was no longer impenetrable.

return unto judgment,' and it obtain, by virtue of its excellence, final victory and perfect peace.[3]

During this period certain persons were apparently making a number of criticisms about Christianity. In sum, the Christian faith was seen as antithetical to good citizenship in the present. How could someone who saw all persons as fellow image-bearers and saw fellow Christians as a spiritual 'brother' or 'sister' give meaningful allegiance to their own particular and earthly city? How could someone who believed his *true* citizenship was to be found in some *heavenly* city be able to be a good citizen in *this* city?[4]

In response to these and related questions, Augustine writes that he has 'things to say in confutation of those who refer the disasters of the Roman republic to our religion, because it prohibits the offering of sacrifices to the gods.' That is, another argument against Christians was that they were coming into conflict with the gods, who demanded certain sacrifices. Augustine goes on to write:

> For this end I must recount all, or as many as may seem sufficient, of the disasters which befell that city and its subject provinces, before these sacrifices were prohibited; for all these disasters they would doubtless have attributed to us, if at that time our religion had shed its light upon them, and had prohibited their sacrifices. I must then go on to show what social wellbeing the true God, in whose hand are all kingdoms, vouchsafed to grant to them that their empire might increase. I must show why He did so, and how their false gods, instead of at all aiding them, greatly injured them by guile and deceit. And, lastly, I must meet those who, when on this point convinced by irrefragable proofs, endeavor to maintain that they worship the gods, not

3   *City of God* I. Preface.

4   See Ernest Fortin, 'Civitate Dei, De,' in *Augustine Through the Ages*, ed. Allan D. Fitzgerald (Grand Rapids: Eerdmans, 1999), 197.

hoping for the present advantages of this life, but for those which are to be enjoyed after death.[5]

Augustine spends Books 1–10 laying out his critique of various pagan arguments against Christianity. Then, in Books 11–22 he outlines (at great length!) 'the origin, history, and deserved ends of the two cities.'[6] We will work this out below, but in sum, the two cities are (1) the city of God and (2) the city of man. Or, one might say, the two cities are (1) those persons who are Christians and (2) those persons who will never become Christians. But there is another sense of the two cities which shows up at times. The two cities can be (1) those spiritual activities and realities and (2) those more worldly or secular activities. That is, in this last sense, the two cities can at times be virtually be (1) *spiritual* versus (2) *worldly* realms.

Augustine's arguments against the pagans are manifold. At times he uses rather straightforward logical argument and historical analysis. For instance, Rome suffered many attacks and evils *before* Christianity was the dominant religion. Rome had never been able to truly achieve justice, even *before* Christianity emerged. The Roman gods have logged a long and sordid track record of capriciousness and pettiness and immorality.[7] Augustine summarizes Books II and III as follows:

> We had promised, then, that we would say something against those who attribute the calamities of the Roman republic to our religion, and that we would recount the evils, as many and great as we could remember or might deem sufficient, which that city, or the provinces belonging to its empire, had suffered before their sacrifices were prohibited, all of which would beyond doubt have been attributed to us, if our religion had

---

5 *City of God* I.36.

6 *Ibid.*, X.32.

7 These arguments are found in Books II and III of *The City of God*.

either already shone on them or had thus prohibited their sacrilegious rites.[8]

Augustine also notes that in many ways Christianity has been *good* for the city of Rome. Thus Augustine asserts that when barbarians attacked Rome many Romans survived because they took refuge in Christian churches, which—Augustine argues—the barbarians refused to attack.[9]

Augustine also argues (Book IV) that the only reason *any* city—including Rome—achieves any success or stability of happiness is due to the providential workings of God. Augustine writes about 'how much succor God, through the name of Christ, to whom the barbarians beyond the custom of ward paid so much honor, has bestowed on the good and bad, according as it is written, "Who maketh His sun to rise on the good and the evil, and giveth rain to the just and the unjust."'[10]

Augustine is concerned to show in *The City of God* the nature of the two cities, and their interrelationship. While 'success' and 'failure' in the earthly realm cannot always be directly related to human obedience and disobedience, nonetheless, blessing often does follow obedience. Augustine writes of the 'successful' Roman leader, and suggests that his success may have been greater if he had followed the one true God.[11]

Ultimately, for Augustine, God sovereignly reigns over all kingdoms: 'God can never be believed to have left the kingdoms of men, their dominations and servitudes, outside of the laws of His providence.'[12] Likewise:

[W]e do not attribute the power of giving kingdoms and empires to any save to the true God, who gives happiness in the

---

8   *Ibid.*, IV.2.

9   *Ibid.*, I.1.

10   *Ibid.*, IV.2.

11   *Ibid.*, IV.28.

12   *Ibid.*, V.11.

kingdom of heaven to the pious alone, but gives kingly power on earth both to the pious and the impious, as it may please Him, whose good pleasure is always just.[13]

Even wars are subject to the sovereign will of God: 'Thus also the durations of wars are determined by Him as He may see meet, according to His righteous will, and pleasure, and mercy, to afflict or console the human race, so that they are sometimes of longer, sometimes of shorter duration.'[14]

Augustine summarizes his overarching purpose for *The City of God* as follows:

> In truth, these two cities are entangled together in this world, and intermixed until the last judgment effect their separation. I now proceed to speak, as God shall help me, of the rise, progress, and end of these two cities; and what I write, I will write for the glory of the city of God, that, being placed in comparison with the other, it may shine with a brighter luster.[15]

Two Cities, Two Loves

In Book XI of *The City of God* Augustine begins to trace out 'the origin, history, and destinies of the two cities, the earthly and the heavenly.'[16] Augustine, of course, finds the imagery for the 'city of God' from Scripture itself. He makes recourse to Psalm 87:3: 'Glorious things are spoken of thee, O city of God' (KJV); Psalm 48:1-2: 'Great is the Lord, and greatly to be praised in the city of our God, in the mountain of His holiness, increasing the joy of the whole earth' (KJV); and Psalm 46:4-5: 'There is a river, the streams whereof shall make glad the city of our God, the holy place of the tabernacles of the most High. God is in the midst of her, she shall not be moved' (KJV). In the opening

---

13   *Ibid.*, V.21.

14   *Ibid.*, V.22.

15   *Ibid.*, I.35.

16   *Ibid.*, XI. Argument.

section of Book XI, Augustine writes these summative words about the two cities:

> I will endeavor to treat of the origin, and progress, and deserved destinies of the two cities (the earthly and the heavenly, to wit), which, as we said, are in this present world commingled, and as it were entangled together. And, first, I will explain how the foundations of these two cities were originally laid, in the difference that arose among the angels.[17]

What are the two 'cities'? The answer may be a little more complicated than is first supposed, for the definitions can shift a bit throughout *The City of God*, as well as throughout Augustine's other writings. At times the 'earthly city' denotes the typical affairs of this temporal realm: politics, for example.[18] At other times, the 'heavenly city' represents Christians, while the 'earthly city' often means something like the lost/unsaved/reprobate. For example, Augustine can write:

> [T]here are no more than two kinds of human society, which we may justly call two cities, according to the language of our Scriptures. The one consists of those who wish to live after the flesh, the other of those who wish to live after the spirit; and when they severally achieve what they wish, they live in peace, each after their kind.[19]

The two cities are intermingled in the present:

> During the present age these two cities are mingled together, but they will be separated at the end. They are in conflict with each other, one fighting on behalf of iniquity, the other for justice; one for what is worthless, the other for truth. This mixing together in the present age sometimes brings it about that certain persons who belong to the city of Babylon are in

---

17 *Ibid.*, XI.1.

18 This is the meaning in Exposition on the Psalms 61 (verse 8).

19 *Ibid.*, XIV.1.

charge of affairs that concern Jerusalem, or, again, that some who belong to Jerusalem administer the business of Babylon.[20]

The two cities have their origin—ultimately—in Adam himself. For at first there was only the city of God, and no earthly city—for the earthly city only truly comes into being with sin. Augustine writes:

> [I]n this first man, who was created in the beginning, there was laid the foundation, not indeed evidently, but in God's foreknowledge, of these two cities or societies, so far as regards the human race. For from that man all men were to be derived—some of them to be associated with the good angels in their reward, others with the wicked in punishment; all being ordered by the secret yet just judgment of God.[21]

Love is at the heart of understanding what distinguishes the two cities, and Augustine makes a fascinating argument about Rome (as one instantiation of the earthly city) and the Church (as the heavenly city). Augustine writes: 'Rome, after it had been built and dedicated, worshipped its founder in a temple as a god; but this Jerusalem laid Christ, its God, as its foundation, that the building and dedication might proceed. The former [Rome] loved its founder, and therefore believed him to be a god; the latter [the church] believed Christ to be God, and therefore loved Him.'[22] Indeed, Romulus (ostensibly the founder of Rome) serves for Augustine as a type of foil against which to delineate the divinity and majesty of Christ.[23]

At the heart of the two cities are two loves. At the very end of Book XIV of *The City of God* Augustine gives perhaps the clearest summary of how the two cities are most centrally

20   *Expositions on the Psalms* 61 (verse 5).

21   *City of God* XII.27.

22   *Ibid.*, XXII.6.

23   *Ibid.*

rooted in two loves: either (1) love of self or (2) love of God.[24] Augustine can also speak of the two cities as (1) the redeemed who trust Christ and (2) the lost who will never trust Christ. He says, 'The [human] race we have distributed into two parts, the one consisting of those who live according to man, the other of those who live according to God. And these we also mystically call the two cities, or the two communities of men, of which the one is predestined to reign eternally with God, and the other to suffer eternal punishment with the devil.'[25] All of history can be understood in terms of the origin, growth, and end of these two cities: 'For this whole time or world-age, in which the dying give place and those who are born succeed, is the career of these two cities concerning which we treat.'[26]

All persons start their lives as part of the earthly city, and through grace each can be brought into the city of God: 'Now citizens are begotten to the earthly city by nature vitiated by sin, but to the heavenly city by grace freeing nature from sin; whence the former are called "vessels of wrath," the latter "vessels of mercy."'[27]

While I have suggested above that Augustine can define the 'two cities' in different ways throughout his writings, it is nonetheless the case that Augustine consistently teaches that the earthly city comes to end, while the heavenly city does not. Thus, the earthly city 'shall not be everlasting ... when it has been committed to the extreme penalty.'[28]

Ultimately the true founder of the earthly city is Cain, who founds the earthly city in slaying his brother.[29] There are thus two lines—one proceeding from Cain (the earthly city) and one

---

24   Ibid., XIV.28.

25   Ibid., XV.1.

26   Ibid.

27   Ibid., XV.2.

28   Ibid., XV.4.

29   Ibid., XV.5–8.

proceeding from Seth (the heavenly city), and these two lines constitute the two cities.[30] Adam is then the father of these 'two lines, proceeding from two fathers, Cain and Seth, and in those sons of theirs whom it behooved to register, the tokens of the two cities began to appear more distinctly.'[31]

These two cities, then, both start 'from a common gate opened in Adam,' and then proceed to run on to their 'proper and merited ends.' Both cities have a temporal component (they exist in the here and now). The earthly city will come to an end in judgment, while the heavenly city will continue on for eternity (and the heavenly city for the present 'sojourns on earth').[32]

The two cities run parallel courses throughout history, and 'both cities, in their course amid mankind, certainly experienced chequered times together just as from the beginning.'[33] The members of the two cities are compared to different fish that swim together in the sea: 'Many of the reprobate are mixed in with the good. Both are gathered, so to speak, in the nets of the Gospel, and in this world, as in the sea, both swim about without distinction, enclosed in those nets until drawn to the shore, where the evil will be separated from the good and "God may be all in all" (1 Cor. 15:28) in the good as in His temple.'[34]

Citizens of the heavenly city (while sojourning in the earthly city) are to call persons out of the earthly city. As Augustine writes: 'This heavenly city, then, while it sojourns on earth, calls citizens out of all nations, and gathers together a society of pilgrims of all languages, not scrupling about diversities in the manners, laws, and institutions whereby earthly peace is secured and maintained, but recognizing that, however various these are,

---

30 *Ibid.*, XV.8.

31 *Ibid.*, XV.17.

32 *Ibid.*, XV.21.

33 *Ibid.*, XVIII.1.

34 *Ibid.*, XVIII.49.

they all tend to one and the same end of earthly peace.'[35] The heavenly city can benefit from the peace found in, and provided by, the earthly city, but the citizens of the heavenly city must always remember that true peace is ultimately only found in 'the perfectly ordered and harmonious enjoyment of God and of one another in God.'[36]

The 'two cities,' then, can be understood as one way of simply tracing out the history of redemption. To call Augustine's *The City of God* a 'philosophy of history' may be true enough, but it may be better to see this key work as Augustine's way of tracing out the history of redemption. This in fact may be the best way to think about a 'philosophy of history.' That is, instead of thinking of 'history' (in an almost 'neutral' or 'secular' sense), and then thinking of God's actions in history as a supplement to 'neutral' or 'secular' history, it is probably better to think of all of history as encompassed within the more fundamental story of the history of redemption—which Augustine traces out in terms of the two cities.[37]

The End of the City of God

Augustine teaches that the end of the city of God is eternal blessedness. Augustine spends a large portion of the last book of *The City of God* (Book XXII) dealing with this state of blessedness. Key to this final state is, of course, the resurrection. In the resurrection all of the inhabitants of the city of God will be raised up and transformed such that there is no deformity, and that all is in perfect proportion. Indeed, Augustine writes:

> Anything misshapen will be set right; anything smaller than is fitting will be supplemented from resources known to the

---

35   *Ibid.*, XIX.17.

36   *Ibid.*

37   For a very helpful way of getting into these kinds of issues, one might turn to Cornelius Van Til, *Common Grace and the Gospel*, revised edition, ed. K. Scott Oliphant (Philadelphia: Presbyterian and Reformed Publishing, 2015).

creator; and anything larger than is fitting will be removed, but with the integrity of the material preserved.[38]

In short, there is continuity between our pre-resurrection and post-resurrection bodies (i.e., it really is the same body), but there is also discontinuity in that there is a perfecting and transforming of the body.[39] This transformation of the body—due to the power of God—will even include bodies or body parts that have disintegrated (or, for example, which have been cremated).[40]

Man's end for Augustine is to one day see God face to face. This insight lies at the heart of *The Trinity*, as seen above, and it is found—fittingly—at the end of *The City of God*. First Corinthians 13:12 is key: 'For now we see in a mirror dimly, but then face to face. Now I know in part; then I shall know fully, even as I have been fully known.' Augustine is reticent to speculate at any length about the exact nature of such heavenly 'vision': 'But whether they will see him by means of the body—as we now see the sun, the moon, the stars, the sea, the earth, and the things on the earth—is no small question.'[41]

In the future city of God there shall be an 'eternal blessedness,' and Augustine makes the provocative suggestion that we will make 'great and marvelous discoveries,' and these discoveries shall 'kindle rational minds in praise of the great Artificer,' and there shall be 'the enjoyment of a beauty which appeals to the reason.' Rather than play reason and beauty against each other (as is sometimes done today), the beauty we see and experience in the city of God in the future shall actually 'appeal' to reason.[42]

---

38   *City of God* XXII.19.

39   *Ibid.*

40   *Ibid.*, XXII.20.

41   *Ibid.*, XXII.29.

42   *Ibid.*, XXII.30.

This future knowledge 'shall be perfected when we shall be perfectly at rest, and shall perfectly know that He is God.'[43]

All through Augustine's thought, he emphasizes the centrality of our desires (whether for good or bad), and he returns to this at the end of *City of God*. In the end our ultimate desire is for God, so it is fitting that God be radically present in the future heavenly city: 'He [God] shall be the end of our desires who shall be seen without end, loved without cloy, praised without weariness.'[44]

In this future state it is most certainly the case that free will is *not* lacking. Rather, '[The will] will, on the contrary, be all the more truly free, because set free from delight in sinning to take unfailing delight in not sinning.'[45] Hence while the first man—Adam before the fall—had *posse non peccare* (the ability *not* to sin) and *posse peccare* (the ability *to* sin), in our future and heavenly state we shall be *non posse peccare* (not able to sin). As Augustine argues, being unable to sin does not mean one is not free. Indeed: 'Are we to say that God Himself is not free because He cannot sin?' 'Free will' indeed will be a reality in heaven: 'In that city, then, there shall be free will, one in all the citizens, and indivisible in each, delivered from all ill, filled with all good, enjoying indefeasibly the delights of eternal joys, oblivious of sins, oblivious of sufferings, and yet not so oblivious of its deliverance as to be ungrateful to its Deliverer.'[46]

Augustine and the Nature of Civil Authority

The Emergence of Civil Government

The City of God is also an important work for understanding Augustine's understanding of the role and nature of civil

43   *Ibid.*
44   *Ibid.*, XXII.29.
45   *Ibid.*, XXII.30.
46   *Ibid.*

government. Augustine argues that civil government is not necessarily sinful, but the need for it emerges only due to sin. God's intention was not that man should rule over man, but the man should simply rule over the rest of the created order:

> He did not intend that His rational creature, who was made in His image, should have dominion over anything but the irrational creation—not man over man, but man over the beasts. And hence the righteous men in primitive times were made shepherds of cattle rather than kings of men, so intending thus to teach us what the relative position of the creatures is, and what the desert of sin.[47]

The Good Ruler and the Good Society

Augustine suggests that there are three key realms (besides the Church) that must be considered when speaking of temporal realms: the house, the city, and the world.[48] Augustine contends that all three realms are related. Thus, the Christian is commanded to love God and neighbor. There is a duty to evangelize my neighbor, ultimately, which springs from the command to love God. As Augustine writes:

> [I]t follows that [the Christian] must endeavor to get his neighbour to love God, since he is ordered to love his neighbor as himself. He ought to make this endeavor on behalf of this wife, his children, his household, all within his reach, even as he would wish his neighbor to do the same for him if he needed it; and consequently he will be at peace, or in well-ordered concord, with all men, as far as in him lies. And this is the order of this concord, that a man, in the first place, injure no one, and, in the second, do good to everyone he can reach.[49]

---

47   Ibid., XIX.15.

48   Ibid., XIX.7.

49   Ibid., XIX.14.

Augustine goes on to suggest that the *first* thing a Christian man must do (in terms of relating to others besides God) is to care for his family. And Augustine delineates this in terms of what is best for the other two realms mentioned above: the city and the world. Thus Augustine writes:

> Primarily, therefore, his own household are his care, for the law of nature and of society gives him readier access to them and greater opportunity of serving them.... But in the family of the just man who lives by faith and is as yet a pilgrim journeying on to the celestial city, even those who rule serve those whom they seem to command; for they rule not from a love of power, but from a sense of the duty they owe to others—not because they are proud of authority, but because they love mercy.[50]

For Augustine, the faithful man is called to serve his family. This is his first duty, and through it he fulfills his duty to the city and the world.

The Authority and Nature of the Government of the Earthly City

Augustine distinguishes between the peace of the earthly city and the peace of the heavenly city. When he does so, he is using 'earthly city' in the sense of the authorities and structures of this temporal realm. Thus he writes:

> The earthly city, which does not live by faith, seeks an earthly peace, and the end it proposes, in the well-ordered concord of civic obedience and rule, is the combination of men's wills to attain the things which are helpful to this life.[51]

The heavenly city is different: 'The heavenly city, or rather the part of it which sojourns on earth and lives by faith, makes use of this peace only because it must, until this mortal condition

---

50   *Ibid.*
51   *Ibid.*, XIX.17.

which necessitates it shall pass away.'[52] And while the heavenly city is sojourning amidst the earthly city, the citizens of the heavenly city are fine to obey the laws of the earthly city (within proper limits):

> Consequently, so long as it [i.e., the city of God, or the inhabitants of the city of God] lives like a captive and a stranger in the earthly city, though it has already received the promise of redemption, and the gift of the Spirit as the earnest of it, it makes no scruple to obey the laws of the earthly city, whereby the things necessary for the maintenance of this mortal life are administered; and thus, as this life is common to both cities, so there is a harmony between them in regard to what belongs to it.[53]

Augustine and Just War

When the notion of 'just war' is broached, it is appropriate to bring Augustine into the discussion. However, it is important to note that Augustine did not write a treatise *per se* on 'just war' and his thoughts must be culled from his various works.

For Augustine, war arises due to sin, even if there are times where it is 'just' to engage in war. Augustine is critical of those who think of war in a flippant way, and do not realize the horror of war. In Book XIX of *The City of God*, Augustine's hypothetical interlocutor says that the wise man will wage just wars. Augustine does not deny this, but he expresses concern about someone not grasping the misery of war. Augustine writes:

> But, say they, the wise man will wage just wars. As if he would not all the rather lament the necessity of just wars, if he remembers that he is a man; for if they were not just he would not wage them, and would therefore be delivered from all wars. For it is the wrong-doing of the opposing party which compels the wise man to wage just wars; and this wrong-doing,

52   *Ibid.*

53   *Ibid.*

even though it gave rise to no war, would still be matter of grief to man because it is man's wrongdoing. Let everyone, then, who thinks with pain on all these great evils, so horrible, so ruthless, acknowledge that this is misery. And if any one either endures or thinks of them without mental pain, this is a more miserable plight still, for he thinks himself happy because he has lost human feeling.[54]

Somewhat analogous to his understanding of the reality of civil government, for Augustine war was certainly *the result of sin*, even if war itself would not always *necessarily* be sinful.

While 'just war theory' as it develops in Western thought has its seeds (in part) in the thought of Augustine, Augustine—unlike much of the later tradition—wrestled at great length with both the Bible itself and the reality of war. The *real* issue is not actually death *per se*, for all persons die. The real issue is the 'lust for domination' (*libido dominandi*).[55] Augustine appeals to John the Baptist's words in Luke 3:14 (where He gives guidance to soldiers) to show that being a soldier can be a just and right vocation for a Christian,[56] and he also turns to Matthew 22:21 (rendering to Caesar what is Caesar's) to show that Christians—through taxes—can legitimately support (i.e., fund) the activities of soldiers.

While war can be legitimate, it is not to be undertaken by the individual or an ad hoc group of individuals, according to Augustine. Rather, war should only be waged by a just and civil authority.[57] But even when a civil government wages war, it needs to be recognized that such authority is derivative—for the civil government's authority comes from God, and the civil government is subservient to God.[58] Thus, when faced

---

54 *Ibid.*

55 *Contra Faustum* XXII.74.

56 *Ibid.*

57 *Ibid.* XXII.75.

58 *Ibid.*

with making sense of the command to turn the other cheek (Matt. 5:39), Augustine has recourse to the 'intention' or 'heart' (turning the other cheek), rather than the 'act' itself, or 'body' (the actual use of force).[59] We should not take delight in vengeance, and even when one must use force, there should be 'benevolence of the will' —even towards the object of force.[60] As Augustine writes:

> [I]f this earthly state keeps the Christian commandments, even wars will not be waged without goodwill in order more easily to take into account the interests of the conquered with a view to a society made peaceful with piety and justice.[61]

It is hard to overestimate the influence of Augustine in these areas. The influence of his *The City of God* is virtually immense— whether on thinking about the nature of history or about how to grasp the significance of life in the world as seen against our ultimate destiny. His thinking about statecraft and war is influential to the very present, even if thinking about 'just war' is now much more secularized, and his insistence on truly loving one's enemies—even in the midst of war—would likely be met by puzzled looks by many moderns. Nonetheless, Augustine's shadow looms large in our day—even amongst those who might not recognize or know much about who is casting the shadow.

---

59   *Ibid.*, XXII.76; *Letter* 138.13.

60   *Letter* 138.14.

61   *Ibid.*

9

AUGUSTINE AND THE PROTESTANT

It is appropriate to end this volume with a few reflections on how a Protestant might appropriate Augustine. I have suggested that there would roughly be three types of Protestant responses to Augustine, depending on the issue:

1. At times the Protestant will find in Augustine a way of articulating things that can be appropriated with little change or concern.
2. At times the Protestant will find in Augustine a way of articulating things that is more puzzling or troubling, and must be re-worked before really being appropriated.
3. At times the Protestant will find in Augustine a way of articulating things which really should not and cannot be appropriated.

This is undoubtedly over-simplified, but it gives a (hopefully reliable) framework for coming to terms with Augustine.

Let us turn to a few of the key issues.

Augustine and the Reality of Sin and Grace

It is with Augustine's doctrines of sin and grace that we find the main line of continuity between Augustine and the Protestant tradition. At the risk of being tendentious and inflammatory, there is something of a line that can be drawn from Paul to Augustine to the Reformation. When Augustine speaks of the *priority, efficacy, life-transforming,* and *perseverance-producing nature of grace,* his way of thinking truly comes to flower in the Protestant Reformation. When Augustine labors at length against the Pelagians to argue that God's work of grace is that which *leads to* good works, and that it is *not* good works which somehow lead to God's grace, he is speaking in terms which will ring true to the Reformation.

And, of course, Augustine's doctrine of sin and the reality of what it means to be fallen rings true and is echoed by the heart of the Protestant Reformation. My own conviction is that the Protestant and Calvinistic/Reformed tradition can lay claim to being the truer heir of Augustine on the questions of sin and grace. We cannot linger here, but there is still work to be done on drawing out the relationship of Augustine to Calvin to Pascal.[1] Pascal, a seventeenth-century Catholic, was in fundamental agreement with the Jansenists (over against the Jesuits). With the victory of the Jesuits over the Jansenists, the true Augustinian doctrine of sin and grace was in many ways lost in Roman Catholicism.

Augustine on Nature and Grace

Augustine's criticisms of Pelagius in *Nature and Grace* are criticisms that could be levied—perhaps with some qualification—at strands of Roman Catholicism today. To the extent to which the Nature-Grace relationship in current Roman Catholic thought stresses *continuity*, there is the danger of a kind of Pelagian error. It is one thing to say that 'nature' *qua* nature is good. It is *another* thing to say that since God made nature by

---

1   Leszek Kolakowski argues that Rome, in condemning Pascal and the Jansenists in the seventeenth century, was essentially condemning their own greatest theologian, Augustine—at least on the doctrines of sin and grace. Cf. Leszek Kolakowski, *God Owes Us Nothing: A Brief Remark on Pascal's Religion and on the Spirit of Jansenism* (Chicago: University of Chicago Press, 1995).

grace, if we do what is in ourselves (i.e. in our 'natural' self), such 'doing' will be recognized or seen as salvific. If grace *simply* 'perfects nature'—without coming to the terms that we are dead in our sins and enemies of God (Rom. 5:10 apart from Christ), then we are dealing with a non-Christian framework which is at its core hostile to the Christian gospel.

One *can*—although carefully—say that 'grace perfects nature.' But it is only nature that has been, and is being, radically redeemed, transformed, and changed, a change flowing from the sacrificial death of Christ on the cross. And this gift of grace has been received by faith alone apart from works, and through this faith we have been brought into an unbreakable covenantal union with the Son, from whom we will never be separated. Interestingly, Augustine can speak of how grace *repairs* rather than *perfects* nature: 'This does not mean that grace has been denied through nature, but rather that nature has been repaired through grace.'[2]

In short, it makes all the difference in the world how we speak of (1) how we come to faith; (2) what faith is and does; (3) how God's grace works in us throughout our lives. Yes, grace 'perfects' us. But in classic Evangelical theology, we are more fallen and in more need than Rome tends to recognize; it also takes a more radical grace to save us than Rome often recognizes. Does 'grace perfect nature?' It depends on a lot more than simply those three words.

Augustine and the Life of the Mind

In contemporary Western culture—including many if not most Christian institutions—we are experiencing a major crisis in terms of thinking about the intellectual life.[3] The Protestant can learn a lot from Augustine. Augustine sows a lot of seeds in his

---

2   *On the Spirit and the Letter* XXVII.47.

3   I have addressed some of these issues in *The Gospel and the Mind: Recovering and Shaping the Intellectual Life* (Wheaton, IL: Crossway, 2010).

writings. These seeds develop and grow in various directions. When a contemporary leader of a Christian school says that 'all truth is God's truth,' 'wherever one finds truth, it is the Lord's,' or that when Christians read non-Christian texts, we should 'plunder the Egyptians,' this person is—with or without knowing it—quoting or paraphrasing Augustine. People like Justin Martyr (A.D. 100–165) could say similar things, but it is Augustine who worked these things out in greater detail. In every act of knowing, it is Christ 'the Teacher'[4] who illumines the mind.

Thomas Aquinas can affirm that 'the human mind stands in need of divine operations, but in knowing natural things it [i.e., the human mind] does *not* require a new light.'[5] Augustine, however, affirms that human knowers *do* need illumination *in every act of knowledge*. I suspect that Augustine's emphasis—when it has been followed in succeeding generations of Western reflection on the life of the mind—has been a bit more successful at guarding against subtle or not-so-subtle attempts at a type of (pretended) intellectual autonomy. That is: because Augustine so emphasized the centrality of Christ the Teacher in every act of human knowing, and Thomas had more room for the human knower knowing at times *without* divine illumination, those who more faithfully followed Augustine have been (generally) able to avoid the temptation of a pretended intellectual autonomy. To put my cards on the table: I believe that in the more Calvinistic and Reformed tradition, there has been (at times!) greater success in continuing to affirm the God-centered and Christ-illuminated nature of the intellectual life, and there has been better success at

---

4   As noted earlier, Augustine devoted a whole treatise to the question of words, signs, and illumination: *The Teacher*.

5   Thomas Aquinas, *The Exposition of Boethius's* On the Trinity, Question I, Article I, Response. This work can be found in *Thomas Aquinas: Selected Writings*, edited and translated by Ralph McInerny (Penguin Books, 1998), 113. My emphasis.

resisting the siren song and allure of the temptation of modernist and Enlightenment notions of intellectual autonomy.[6]

Augustine and the City of God

For a long time I have thought that in many ways Augustine's reflections in *The City of God* foreshadow the contemporary emphasis on trying to grasp in Holy Scripture the nature and contours of the history of redemption.[7] Irenaeus had done this well before in his *Proof of the Apostolic Preaching*—which would have been a wonderful textbook in a second century 'Biblical Theology' course. Augustine, like Irenaeus before him, as well as the fruitful discipline of Biblical Theology in evangelical circles,[8] saw the Bible as displaying a coherent and beautiful history of redemption. Augustine could look at this history as the story of the origin, development, and end of the two cities. Christians can learn much from Augustine at this point. If Scripture really is what Scripture purports to be—the Word of God written—does

---

6   There is more to be said here. My own reading is that even if Thomas did not want his successors to drift toward notions of intellectual autonomy, at least two things have made it difficult for those in the Thomist tradition: (1) a less than fully adequate doctrine of sin, including the radical and disastrous reality of the noetic effects of the fall; (2) given Thomas' denial of the necessity of illumination in every act of knowing, there has been the temptation to in *effect* or in *reality* tend to think of the intellectual life (at times) in a quasi-autonomous sense.

7   See the following footnote.

8   When I speak of 'the history of redemption' and 'Biblical Theology,' these terms can be used in various senses. In particular, I am thinking of that tradition flowing from Donald Robinson, Graeme Goldsworthy, and William Dumbrell from Moore College, as well as Geerhardus Vos before them. These streams of thinkers are now bearing fruit in many efforts, including the dozens of books which can be found in InterVarsity Press' *New Studies in Biblical Theology* series, under the editorship of Donald A. Carson. I would encourage readers wanting to engage the issue of a redemptive-historical hermeneutic to read Richard B. Gaffin, Jr.'s *By Faith, Not by Sight*. Then perhaps read Gaffin's excellent chapter 'The Redemptive-Historical View' in *Biblical Hermeneutics: Five Views*, eds. Stanley E. Porter and Beth Stovall (Downers Grove, IL: IVP Academic, 2012), 89–110. Finally, Cornelius Van Til's *Common Grace and the Gospel* takes up this redemptive-historical framework (generally, and following on from Geerhardus Vos), and applies it to questions of common grace and apologetics.

it not make sense that the story of creation, fall, redemption, and consummation is not simply *a* story, but ultimately *the* story of God, man, and the world? Augustine has bequeathed to the world an example of how to think of the history of all things as ultimately the history of God, man, and the world.

But we might add a more specific repercussion of Augustine's labors. In working through the question of the origin, development, and end of the two cities, Augustine engaged in the theological task with a firm commitment to *history*. It is worth pondering: *if Western theological thought had truly followed Augustine with his thorough emphasis on history and on the importance of history*, would Western theology had looked different over time? An insight from the Dutch philosopher Herman Dooyeweerd might help here.[9] Dooyeweerd suggested that Western culture tended to embrace one of several 'ground-motives.'[10] One might think of these 'ground-motives' as something like 'fundamental frameworks' or the like. As Dooyeweerd sees it, there have been four basic 'ground-motives' in Western history. They are:

1. The *Greek* form-matter motive
2. The *scholastic* nature-grace motive
3. The *humanistic* nature-freedom motive
4. The radical *biblical* motive: creation, fall, redemption, consummation

We can only briefly summarize these points here. But, the *Greek* 'form-matter motive' places an emphasis on form and matter (whether with more Platonic or Aristotelian version). The *scholastic* nature-grace motive places an emphasis on questions of nature and grace, and is seen especially in Roman Catholicism's

---

9   Dooyeweerd was a philosopher in the Netherlands who lived from 1894 to 1977. He was brilliant, and thus can be a tad difficult to read. His *magnum opus* is *New Critique of Theoretical Thought*. For the reader wanting a way into Dooyeweerd, I would recommend his *In the Twilight of Western Thought: Studies in the Pretended Autonomy of Philosophical Thought* (Paideia Press / Reformational Publishing Project, 2012).

10   Dooyeweerd also liked to coin new terms to describe what he was trying to say!

emphasis on a continuity between the two. The *humanistic* nature-freedom motive places an emphasis on questions of what something is ('nature'), and what it means to be free. All three of these 'ground-motives' are ultimately religious, and have their own idols. And those trapped in these ground-motives tend to oscillate from one end of the pole to another—thus between 'form' and 'matter,' or between 'nature' and 'grace,' or between 'nature' and 'freedom.' The *biblical* 'ground-motive' of creation, fall, redemption, consummation, is the only adequate motive, as Dooyeweerd sees it. This (biblical) ground-motive manages to avoid the confused (and idolatrous) problems of the first three.[11]

My main point is simply this: Dooyeweerd's fourth, and biblical, option, or 'ground-motive,' shares with Augustine a thorough interest in history, and in understanding history in explicitly Christian/biblical terms. Augustine speaks of the origin, development, and end of the two cities, whereas Dooyeweerd speaks of creation, fall, redemption, and consummation. Does Western theology at times lose such a biblical emphasis, whether in (1) the *Greek* form-matter motive, or (2) the *scholastic* nature-grace motive, or (3) the *humanistic* nature-freedom motive? If Augustine's (and this may appear anachronistic) historical-redemptive, or creation/fall/redemption/consummation trajectory had been more fully followed and developed, later Western theology would have perhaps looked quite different.

Augustine and Justification

Finally, it is worth bringing things to an end with a brief word on Augustine on justification. Augustine is rightly called the Doctor of Grace. He bequeaths to the Christian Church many rich words and the importance, priority, and efficacy of grace. On that score, the Protestant tradition is in significant debt to Augustine. Thus, it is interesting for the reader or student to

---

11   This is a very short introduction. One can read Dooyeweerd himself, and both John Frame and Ronald Nash have written penetrating critiques of Dooyeweerd. Dooyeweerd is a stimulating thinker, but I would read him with a discerning eye.

try to come to terms with Augustine on justification. Could it be that the Doctor of Grace was out of step with what Martin Luther called 'the doctrine on which the church stands or falls,' or what John Calvin called, 'the hinge of religion'?

I have suggested above that Augustine clearly wished to affirm that it is always God's sovereign grace that leads to faith, and that faith then leads to work or obedience. God's grace never comes to us because of foreseen merit. God's grace is not 'triggered' because of someone's works. And, repeatedly, for Augustine, while the Christian does manifest his or her faith in and through works, *these works always flow from faith.* Additionally, Augustine repeatedly speaks of justification using the perfect, passive, participle: *having been justified.* And there is very often a punctiliar, legal, and declarative sense to justification in Augustine. In short, Augustine gets a lot of things right when he speaks of justification.[12]

Conclusion

At the end of the day, we stand on the shoulders of giants. One of the giants of giants is undoubtedly Augustine. Protestants and Catholics will continue to read him and mine his works, which is as it should be. He built the edifice of Western theology, and one simply cannot grasp the nature and contour of Western theology without going through Augustine.

For good or for ill, it is probably true that all (at least Western) theology is a long series of footnotes to Augustine. Persons trying to think through the radical nature of sin, and how

---

12 See my *Covenant and Commandment: Works, Obedience, and Faithfulness in the Christian Life*, New Studies in Biblical Theology (Downers Grove, IL: 2014). I show that many of the great Protestants could affirm: (1) works are an essential part of the Christian life; (2) works are necessary (properly construed!) for ultimate salvation; (3) through faith we experience a two-fold grace (justification and sanctification—this especially in John Calvin); (4) works are a means, or cause, of ultimate salvation. I attempt to show that these kinds of truths are found in John Calvin, John Owen, Francis Turretin, Jonathan Edwards, as well as in many contemporary thinkers, including Richard B. Gaffin, Jr.

profoundly the lost person is actually *lost*, will be helped in their understanding of the gravity of the fallen human condition. He will continue to be a source of encouragement for Protestants, especially in his understanding and articulation of the deep and life-transforming nature of the grace of God. He will continue to inspire those who discover his conversion story, how a man wrestling deeply and profoundly with sin was sovereignly and radically met by Jesus Christ. Persons seeking to understand something of how to think of the intellectual life in our day will continue to discover his writing on the nature of language and the nature of illumination. And persons trying to understand how a sovereign God relates to the twists and turns of history will return again and again to his *magnum opus*, *The City of God*, which has so shaped (especially) Western reflection on life in this world, while journeying to our truer city.

If you have read this book, now put it down. Go find some Augustine and take up and read. You will not regret it.

FURTHER READING: PRIMARY SOURCES

If you have made it to the end of this book, you may be ready to read some more—and especially to read some Augustine himself. Below I name some of the better translations of Augustine's Latin into English.

Collections of Works. Though a number of collections and series contain the writings of Augustine in English, none contain *all* of them. The publisher New City Press is currently aiming to reach this goal, under the editorship of John Rotelle, and they are well on their way to accomplishing it.

Works of Saint Augustine (New City Press). These volumes have very helpful introductory essays and extensive explanatory footnotes. For the English reader who wants to explore the thought of Augustine in greater depth, they are a good place to start. One can purchase at a reasonable price the digital form of this product from Intelex (their 'Past Masters' series). This is now the standard English translation of Augustine—even if for some particular volumes readers will prefer older or other translations. The introductory essays are helpful, very thorough, although not unnecessarily detailed or intimidating to the reader.

Ancient Christian Writers (Westminster, MD: Newman Press). A series of classic Christian texts in English translation only with introductory essays and explanatory footnotes. These notes are not overly technical and can be helpful for the reader wanting better to grasp Augustine.

The Fathers of the Church (Catholic University Press). This series contains a number of Augustine's works in English translation only. Edited by R. J. Deferrari.

Library of Christian Classics (Westminster/John Knox). This series contains English translations of various Christian writers from across the span of Christian history, including:

- *Augustine: Confessions and Enchiridion*
- *Augustine: Earlier Writings* (all or parts of *The Soliloquies, The Teacher, On Free Will, Of True Religion, The Usefulness of Belief, The Nature of the Good, Faith and the Creed,* and *To Simplicianus—Various Questions*)
- *Augustine: Later Works* (parts of *The Trinity*, the complete *The Spirit and the Letter*, and the complete *Ten Homilies on the First Epistle General of St. John*)

A Select Library of the Nicene and Post-Nicene Fathers of the Christian Church (reprinted by Eerdmans in 1994). This collection contains many of Augustine's writings, and while not exhaustive, is still helpful. The translation is dated, but it has served English readers for many years. It is available free online at www.ccel.org via the Christian Classics Ethereal Library.

Cambridge University Press. Cambridge University Press has translated a number of Augustine's works, perhaps most significantly, *The City of God.*

Self-Standing Volumes. There are a number of self-standing or independent translations of Augustine's works that readers may want to obtain. For example, there are translations of *The City of God* (Henry Bettenson's in 1972 and Marcus Dods' in 1954). Similarly, Henry Chadwick's translation of *Confessions* (Oxford University Press, 1991) is excellent, and the edition I still turn to when reading this volume.

If you decide to get some Latin under your belt and devote yourself to engaging Augustine in the original language, there are several options available to you.

Corpus Scriptorum Ecclesiasticorum Latinorum (**CSEL**) (Vienna: Tempsky, 1865–present). An older collection of Christian Latin texts, also available digitally.

Corpus Christianorum. Series Latina (**CCSL**) (Turnhout: Brepels, 1953-present).This series of Latin texts was originally available in printed form, but is now available digitally as well.

Loeb Classical Library (**LCL**) (London: William Heinemann, 1912-present). A number of Augustine's works are included in this series, which features Latin and English on opposing pages.

Patrologiae Cursus Completus, Series Latina (**PL**), ed. J.P. Migne (Paris 1844-64).

For many years this was the main way to access Christian Latin texts. It is now available digitally as the *Patrologia Latina Database* (**PLD**). It is owned by many libraries, but would be cost-prohibitive for most individuals.

CETEDOC *Library of Christian Latin Texts* (**CLCLT**).

This is the most recent attempt to provide digital access to Christian Latin texts. It is certainly cost-prohibitive for virtually any individual, but is a gold-mine for the Latinist or serious Augustine scholar.

Augustinus.it (http://www.augustinus.it/latino/index.htm). Since many of the tools for accessing Augustine in the Latin are cost-prohibitive for individuals, this site is very useful. It does not have all the search capabilities of other databases. Nonetheless, this site does allow you to read all of the Latin texts in the *Patrologia Latina*. This is an Italian website, so the various titles of Augustine's works are in Italian. But if you have a list of the Latin titles handy (e.g., in the opening pages of *Augustine Through the Ages*), it should be no problem to work out the title.

Scripture and Subject Index for Augustine's Collected Works. This is a good place to mention a free and easily accessible resource. New City Press, who is near to completing the task of translating all of Augustine's works into English, has created a Scripture and Subject Index for their edition, *The Works of Saint Augustine: A Translation for the 21st Century*. One can access the index here: https://www.newcitypress.com/free-index-augustine

It is also worth drawing attention to James J. O'Donnell's web page, which is a helpful holding place for many things Augustinian: www.georgetown.edu/faculty/jod/augustine

Where in Augustine Might a Reader Start?

With Augustine it is particularly difficult to say where to start reading. A lot depends on the reader's interests and background. Augustine's *Confessions* is a true classic (I like the Henry Chadwick translation). *The City of God* is a treasure that cannot be mined enough (Bettenson or Dods are both good, as well as the New City Press edition), and do not feel guilty about skipping ahead to Books 11 and 12 if you are eager to get to the heart of Augustine's thought on the 'two cities.'

For a reader who wants a shorter introduction to the 'big picture' of Augustine's thought, I recommend his *Enchiridion* (the New City Press translation is titled *Manual on Faith, Hope, and Love*). In *Enchiridion*, one has access to the heart of Augustine's thought on a number of issues, all within 150 or so pages. Here is a list of some seminal works of Augustine that might serve as a good summary of his thought. I have used the common English titles, with Latin titles in parentheses (and where there is some disagreement I have used the English titles from the tables in *Augustine Through the Ages*):[1]

Against Two Letters of the Pelagians (Contra duas epistulas Pelagianorum)

On Christian Doctrine (de doctrina Christiana)

The City of God (de Civitate Dei)

Confessions (Confessiones)

On the Gift of Perseverance (De dono perseverantiae)

A Handbook on Faith, Hope, and Love (Enchiridion ad Laurentium de fide spe et caritate)

On the Spirit and the Letter (De spiritu et littera)

To Simplicanius (Ad Simplicianum)

The Trinity (De Trinitate)

---

1   One exception. I have, perhaps stubbornly, continued to refer to (what has traditionally been called) *On Christian Doctrine* by that title, instead of the more recent *Teaching Christianity* or *On Christian Teaching*.

FURTHER READING: SECONDARY SOURCES

There is a never-ending and growing list of writings on Augustine. Here are some brief notes on books that I frequently recommend.

Lewis Ayres, *Augustine and the Trinity*. Cambridge: Cambridge University Press, 2014 (softback).

Ayres is one of the finest Augustine scholars around. Anything he writes on Augustine is worth reading.

Gerald Bray, *Augustine on the Christian Life: Transformed by the Power of God*. Wheaton, IL: Crossway Books, 2015.

Bray knows Augustine well, and this is a superb introduction—with special attention given to Augustine's insights and teachings related to practical Christian living.

Peter Brown, *Augustine of Hippo: A Biography*.

This classic biography has come out in several editions. I recommend the 2000 revised edition, from University of California Press, though I might turn to Lancel (below) first.

Henry Chadwick, *A Very Short Introduction to Augustine*. Oxford: Oxford University Press, 2001.

A slim yet very helpful volume by a senior scholar, part of Oxford University Press' 'A Very Short Introduction' series.

Allan D. Fitzgerald, *Augustine Through the Ages: An Encyclopedia.* Grand Rapids: Eerdmans, 1999.

For the person who wants to get to know the thought of Augustine, it would be hard to improve upon the essays in this volume. Take a morning or an afternoon to peruse these essays and read several more thoroughly. The work as a whole has excellent bibliographies.

Andrew Knowles and Pachomios Penkett, *Augustine and His World.* IVP Histories. Downers Grove: InterVarsity Press, 2004.

A wonderful introduction to Augustine, featuring a nice layout with beautiful pictures and art.

Serge Lancel, *St. Augustine*, tr. Antonia Nevill. London: SCM, 2002.

I read this from cover to cover, and have found it to be perhaps one of the best secondary sources available on Augustine in general. Highly recommended.

Bryan Litfin, 'Augustine,' in *Getting to Know the Church Fathers: An Evangelical Introduction.* Grand Rapids: Baker, 2007.

A helpful chapter-length introduction to Augustine that provides an accessible overview.

David Vincent Menconi and Eleonore Stump, eds., *The Cambridge Companion to Augustine.* Second Edition. Cambridge: Cambridge University Press, 2014.

This volume and the first edition below (edited by Eleonore Stump and Norman Kretzmann) are both thorough introductions to various aspects of Augustine's thought.

Ronald N. Nash, *The Light of the Mind: St. Augustine's Theory of Knowledge.* Lexington: University of Kentucky Press, 1969.

This is essentially Nash's doctoral dissertation, and is still the seminal work in the field. Nash has condensed this material into the 'Illumination' entry in *Augustine Through the Ages*.

N. R. Needham, *The Triumph of Grace: Augustine's Writings on Salvation*. London: Grace Publications Trust, 2000.

Needham has provided readers with a true theological treasure, a collection of Augustine's writings on sin, grace, and salvation.

Eleonore Stump and Norman Kretzmann, eds., *The Cambridge Companion to Augustine*. Cambridge: Cambridge University Press, 2001.

Though the second edition is more recent and contains important perspective, the first edition is also worth reading.

BIBLIOGRAPHY

I chose in this book to concentrate mainly on the writings of Augustine himself, and not to spend excessive time adjudicating for the reader the world of Augustine scholarship—which is virtually endless. The following bibliography consists simply of works referenced. For recommended reading, see the previous section.

Aquinas, Thomas. *The Exposition of Boethius's On the Trinity*, Question I, Article I, Response. In *Thomas Aquinas: Selected Writings*. Edited and translated by Ralph McInerny. Penguin Books, 1998.

Blocher, Henri. '*Agnus Victor*: The Atonement as Victory and Vicarious Punishment.' In John G. Stackhouse, Jr., ed., *What Does it Mean To Be Saved? Broadening Evangelical Horizons on Salvation*. Grand Rapids: Baker Book House, 2002. Pages 67-91.

Bourke, Vernon. *The Essential Augustine*. Second Edition. Indianapolis, IN: Hackett Publishing Company, 1974.

Brown, Peter. 'Political Society,' in Richard Markus, ed. *Augustine: A Collection of Critical Essays*. Garden City, N.J.: Doubleday, 1972.

Calvin, John. *Institutes of the Christian Religion.* Two volumes. Edited by John McNeill, and translated by Ford Lewis Battles. Philadelphia: Westminster Press, 1960.

Cutrone, Emmanuel J. 'Sacraments.' In *Augustine Through the Ages: An Encyclopedia.* Edited by Allan D. Fitzgerald. Grand Rapids: Eerdmans, 1999.

Dooyeweerd, Herman. *In the Twilight of Western Thought: Studies in the Pretended Autonomy of Philosophical Thought.* Paideia Press/ Reformational Publishing Project, 2012.

_____. *New Critique of Theoretical Thought.* Phillipsburg, NJ: Presbyterian and Reformed Publishers, 1969.

Eco, Umberto. *Semiotics and the Philosophy of Language.* Bloomington, IN: Indiana University Press, 1984.

Elshtain, Jean Bethke. 'Why Augustine? Why Now?,' in *Augustine and Postmodernism: Confessions and Circumfession,* edited by John D. Caputo and Michael J. Scanlon. Bloomington, IN: Indiana University Press, 2005.

Fitzgerald, Allan D., ed. *Augustine Through the Ages: An Encyclopedia.* Grand Rapids: Eerdmans, 1999.

Fortin, Ernest. 'Civitate Dei, De,' in *Augustine Through the Ages,* ed., Allan D. Fitzgerald. Grand Rapids: Eerdmans, 1999.

Frend, W.H.C. *The Donatist Church: A Movement of Protest in Roman North Africa.* Oxford: Oxford University Press, 1952.

Gilson, Etienne. *The Christian Philosophy of Saint Augustine.* New York: Random House, 1960.

Green, Bradley G. *Covenant and Commandment: Works, Obedience, and Faithfulness in the Christian Life.* New Studies in Biblical Theology. Nottingham, UK: Apollos; Downers Grove, IL: IVP, 2014.

_____. *The Gospel and the Mind: Recovering and Shaping the Intellectual Life.* Wheaton, IL: Crossway, 2010.

Gaffin, Richard B., Jr. 'The Redemptive-Historical View.' In *Biblical Hermeneutics: Five Views*, eds. Stanley E. Porter and Beth Stovall. Downers Grove, IL: IVP Academic, 2012. Pages 89–110.

Gilson, Etienne. *The Christian Philosophy of Saint Augustine.* New York: Random House, 1960.

Harrison, Carol. 'Augustine.' In *The New Cambridge History of the Bible*, vol. 1, *From the Beginnings to 600.* Cambridge: Cambridge University Press, 2013.

Helseth, Paul Kjoss. *'Right Reason' and the Princeton Mind: An Unorthodox Proposal.* Phillipsburg, NJ: Presbyterian and Reformed Publishers, 2010.

Jeffrey, David Lyle. *People of the Book: Christian Identity and Literary Culture.* Grand Rapids: Eerdmans, 1996.

Johnson, Dru. *Biblical Knowing: A Scriptural Epistemology of Error.* Eugene, OR: Cascade Books, 2013.

Kolakowski, Leszek. *God Owes Us Nothing: A Brief Remark on Pascal's Religion and on the Spirit of Jansenism.* Chicago: University of Chicago Press, 1995.

Lancel, Serge. *St. Augustine*, tr. Antonia Nevill. London: SCM, 2002.

Leporcq, J. *Sentiments de saint Augustin sur la grâce* (no publication information given).

Letham, Robert. *The Holy Trinity: In Scripture, History, Theology, and Worship.* Phillipsburg, NJ: Presbyterian and Reformed Publishers, 2004.

de Lubac, Henri. *Augustinianism and Modern Theology*, translated by Louis Dupré. New York: Herder and Herder, 2000.

————————. *Catholicism: Christ and the Common Destiny of Man*. San Francisco: Ignatius Press, 1988.

Markus, R.A. 'Donatus, Donatism.' In *Augustine Through the Ages: An Encyclopedia*. Edited by Allan D. Fitzgerald. Grand Rapids: Eerdmans, 1999.

Mononchak, Joseph A. 'True and Perfect Sacrifice,' in *Commonweal*, March 21, 2015. https://www.commonwealmagazine.org/true-and-perfect-sacrifice

Muller, Richard A. *Dictionary of Latin and Greek Theological Terms*. Second Edition. Grand Rapids: Baker Academic, 2017.

Owen, John. *Communion with the Triune God*. Edited by Kelly Kapic and Justin Taylor. Wheaton, IL: Crossway Books, 2007.

Pelagius. *Pelagius' Commentary on St Paul's Epistle to the Romans*. Oxford Early Christian Studies. Edited by Theodore De Bruyn. Henry Chadwick and Rowan Williams, Series Editors. Oxford: Clarendon Press, 1993.

Pfau, Thomas. *Minding the Modern: Human Agency, Intellectual Traditions, and Responsible Knowledge*. Notre Dame, IN: University of Notre Dame Press, 2013.

Rickaby, Joseph. *Augustine's City of God: A View of the Contents*. Eugene, OR: Wipf and Stock, 2008.

Teske, Roland J. 'Augustine's Use of "*Substantia*" in Speaking About God.' In *The Modern Schoolman* LXII (March 1985): 149.

————————. 'Properties of God and the Predicaments in *The Trinity* V.' In *The Modern Schoolman* LIX (1981): 1–19.

Van Til, Cornelius. *Common Grace and the Gospel*. Revised edition. Edited by K. Scott Oliphint. Philadelphia: Presbyterian and Reformed Publishing, 2015.

————————. 'Nature and Scripture.' In Peter Lillback and Richard B. Gaffin, Jr., *Thy Word Is Still Truth: Essential Writings on the*

Doctrine of Scripture from the Reformation to Today. Phillipsburg, New Jersey: Presbyterian and Reformed Publishers, 2013. Pages 921–41.

Verduin, Leonard. *The Reformers and Their Stepchildren.* Grand Rapids: Eerdmans, 1964.

Warfield, Benjamin Breckenridge. 'Augustine.' In *Calvin and Augustine*, ed. Samuel G. Craig. Philadelphia: The Presbyterian and Reformed Publishing Company, 1956.

_____. 'The Pelagian Controversy.' In *Studies in Tertullian and Augustine*. New York: Oxford University Press, 1930.

Wright, David. 'Justification in Augustine.' In Bruce McCormack, ed., *Justification in Perspective: Historical Developments and Contemporary Challenges*. Grand Rapids: Baker Book House, 2006.

ACKNOWLEDGMENTS

When Michael Haykin asked me several years ago to write a short book on Augustine, I thought, 'Of course I should do this.' Yet, writing a short book on one of the most important figures in the history of Western thought has been difficult. Thank you, Michael, for the opportunity and for your patience. Thank you to co-editor Shawn Wilhite, who has a great eye for detail. Rebecca Rine was a great editor, and I am in her debt for all of her great work. Thank you to all of the folks at Christian Focus for your support of this project. I am appreciative of the Board of Trustees and administration of Union University, who have supported my efforts to research and write. My Dean, Ray Van Neste, and Associate Dean, Jacob Shatzer, have been supporters as well. Thanks, fellows. Parts of this book have been adapted from a chapter I wrote, 'Augustine,' in the book *Shapers of Christian Orthodoxy: Engaging with Early and Medieval Theologians.*[1] My thanks to the publisher of that book, IVP-UK, for permission to reprint. Significant portions of the book were completed at Tyndale House in Cambridge, England. A big thanks to the

---

1   Bradley G. Green, ed. *Shapers of Christian Orthodoxy: Engaging with Early and Medieval Theologians* (Nottingham, UK: IVP-UK; Downers Grove, IL: IVP, 2010), 235–92. A big thanks to Phil Duce with IVP-UK, who published the volume. Used with permission.

folks at Tyndale House, which is simply a great place to research and write. Lewis Ayres and Leonardo De Chirico read the manuscript and shared meaningful feedback. My sincere thanks to these two gentlemen, and again to Leonardo for also writing the Foreword. As this book was in the final stages of editing I had the opportunity to teach a course on Augustine for Bethlehem College and Seminary. A number of students in that class sent me some thoughtful suggestions (and notes on typos). Thank you, gentlemen. I wish to express my thanks to my wife, Dianne, and my children, Caleb, Daniel, and Victoria, who have all been patient and supportive as I have worked on this volume. Finally, this book is dedicated to the families, friends, and founders of Augustine School, a wonderful school in Jackson, Tennessee, where hopefully the legacy of Augustine lives on—albeit in a Protestant key.

More from the Early Church Fathers *series...*

EARLY CHURCH FATHERS
SERIES EDITOR MICHAEL A. G. HAYKIN

PATRICK
OF HIS LIFE & IMPACT
IRELAND

MICHAEL A. G. HAYKIN

ISBN 978-1-5271-0100-5

PATRICK OF IRELAND

Michael A. G. Haykin

Patrick ministered to kings and slaves alike in the culture that had enslaved him. Patrick's faith and his commitment to the Word of God through hard times is a true example of the way that God calls us to grow and to bless those around us through our suffering. Michael Haykin's masterful biography of Patrick's life and faith will show you how you can follow God's call in your life. This series relates the magnificent impact that these fathers of the early church made for our world today.

Michael A. G. Haykin is Professor of Church History and Biblical Spirituality at the Southern Baptist Theological Seminary, Louisville, Kentucky where he is also Director of the Andrew Fuller Center for Baptist Studies. He has written several books and is the series editor of the Early Church Fathers series.

Sometimes the historical figure outshines the legend. By sifting through reliable sources, Michael A. G. Haykin paints a compelling portrait of this bibliocentric bishop and earnest evangelist. The dedicated missionary and thoughtful theologian that emerges belongs to the Gospel-loving global Church and not just the Emerald Isle. The persistent Patrick, a diligent minister of the Word and Spirit, deserves to be commemorated far more than once each year.

Paul Hartog
Adjunct Faculty – Biblical Studies,
Faith Baptist Bible College and Theological Seminary,
Ankeny, Iowa

EARLY CHURCH FATHERS
SERIES EDITORS
MICHAEL A. G. HAYKIN & SHAWN J. WILHITE

BASIL
OF
HIS LIFE
& IMPACT
CAESAREA

MARVIN JONES

ISBN 978-1-5271-0154-8

BASIL OF CAESAREA

MARVIN JONES

Much is known about Basil of Caesarea (329–379)—a Greek Bishop in what is now Turkey. A thoughtful theologian, he was instrumental in the formation of the Nicene Creed and fought a growing heresy, Arianism, which had found converts even in those in high positions of state. In the face of such a threat he showed courage, wisdom and complete confidence in God—without which, the Church would not be what it is today.

Marvin Jones is an Assistant Professor of Church History and Theology at Louisiana College in Pineville, Louisiana. He holds degrees from Southeastern Baptist Theological Seminary, Dallas Theological Seminary and the University of South Africa.

Introduces us not just to the subtlety and real acuity of Basil's thought but to a man of great warmth and affection... challenges us as well as instructs us.

Michael Ovey, (1958-2017)
Principal, Oak Hill Theological College, London

Christian Focus Publications

Our mission statement—STAYING FAITHFUL
In dependence upon God we seek to impact the world through literature faithful to His infallible Word, the Bible. Our aim is to ensure that the Lord Jesus Christ is presented as the only hope to obtain forgiveness of sin, live a useful life and look forward to heaven with Him.

Our Books are published in four imprints:

CHRISTIAN
FOCUS

popular works including biographies, commentaries, basic doctrine and Christian living.

CHRISTIAN
HERITAGE

books representing some of the best material from the rich heritage of the church.

MENTOR

books written at a level suitable for Bible College and seminary students, pastors, and other serious readers. The imprint includes commentaries, doctrinal studies, examination of current issues and church history.

CF4•K

children's books for quality Bible teaching and for all age groups: Sunday school curriculum, puzzle and activity books; personal and family devotional titles, biographies and inspirational stories—Because you are never too young to know Jesus!

Christian Focus Publications Ltd,
Geanies House, Fearn, Ross-shire,
IV20 1TW, Scotland, United Kingdom.
www.christianfocus.com